Building Classroom Success

Also available from Continuum

Building Classroom Success

Eliminating Academic Fear and Failure

ANDREW MARTIN

Teachers' resources to accompany this book are available online at: www.continuumbooks.com/resources/9781847065605
Please visit the link and register with us to receive your password and to access these downloadable resources.
If you experience any problems accessing the resources, please contact Continuum at: info@continuumbooks.com

continuum

Continuum International Publishing Group
The Tower Building   80 Maiden Lane
11 York Road   Suite 704
London   New York
SE1 7NX   NY 10038

www.continuumbooks.com

British Library Cataloguing-in-Publication Data
A catalogue record for this book is available from the British Library.

ISBN: 978-1-84706-560-5 (paperback)

Library of Congress Cataloging-in-Publication Data
Martin, Andrew, 1966–
     Building classroom success: eliminating academic fear and failure/ Andrew Martin.
       p. cm.
     Includes bibliographical references and index.
     ISBN 978-1-84706-560-5 (pbk.)
   1. Effective teaching. 2. Academic achievement. 3. Classroom management. I. Title.

   LB1025.3.M33713   2010
   371.102–dc22

Typeset by BookEns, Royston, Herts.
Printed and bound in Bell & Bain, Glasgow.

Contents

Contents

About the author

Andrew Martin, BA (Hons), MEd (Hons), PhD, is Professor of Educational Psychology at the University of Sydney specializing in motivation, engagement, achievement and quantitative research methods. He is also a Registered Educational and Child Psychologist.

Andrew is widely recognized for his psychological and educational research in achievement motivation. Although the bulk of his research focuses on motivation, engagement and achievement, Andrew has also published in areas such as boys' education, gifted and talented, academic resilience and academic buoyancy, personal bests, pedagogy, parenting, teacher–student relationships and Aboriginal education.

Based on International Rankings of the Most Productive Educational Psychologists (2003–08), Andrew is the ninth most published across all peer-reviewed journals and the most highly published researcher from an Australian university across all peer-reviewed journals (Jones *et al.* (in press) *Contemporary Educational Psychology*).

Andrew has written over 200 peer-reviewed journal articles, chapters and papers in published conference proceedings; written 3 books for parents and teachers (published in 5 languages); compiled 12 commissioned government reports; won 10 Australian Research Council grants and 15 government and non-government research tenders; is Associate Editor of the *Journal of Educational Psychology* and Associate Editor of the *British Journal of Educational Psychology*; is on Editorial Boards of 3 international journals (*American Educational Research Journal, Educational and Psychological Measurement,* and *Contemporary Educational Psychology*); has reviewed for 35 academic journals and numerous international research councils and institutions; has delivered over 100 invited presentations and conference keynotes; and, has conducted workshops in over 100 schools and over 200 radio, television and newspaper interviews.

In 2008 Andrew received the American Educational Research Association (AERA) Early Career Award, 'To recognize a scholar who has conducted a distinguished program of cumulative educational research in any field of educational inquiry within the first decade following receipt of their doctoral degree.' (AERA Awards Program, 2008). Andrew was the sole researcher to win the Award across all AERA Divisions (Administration; Curriculum; Learning and Instruction; Measurement and Methodology; Counselling and Human Development; History; Sociology; Evaluation and Assessment; Professional; Postsecondary; Teacher Education; Policy and Politics). Prior to that Andrew was listed in *The Bulletin* magazine's 'SMART 100 Australians' (2003) and one of only three academics judged to be in the Top 10 in the field of Education in Australia. In 2002, his PhD was judged the Most Outstanding Doctoral Dissertation in Educational Psychology by Division 15 of the American Psychological Association and before that was judged the Most Outstanding PhD in Education in Australia by the Australian Association for Research in Education.

Andrew lives in Sydney, Australia with his wife and two (school) children.

Acknowledgements

My sincere gratitude goes to my wife and children who are a constant source of love, inspiration and instruction. Many thanks to Tara Wynne and Grace Heifetz at Curtis Brown, Australia for their terrific support, guidance and advice over the years and with this book. A special thanks also goes to Continuum and in particular Liz Blackmore, Vivien Ward, Christina Garbutt, and Ania Leslie-Wujastyk who have backed and supported me through the preparation and publication of this book. Mandy Gentle did a marvellous job copyediting the book, sharpening its clarity and focus. Arthur Foulser and staff at BookEns Editorial Services also did a great job preparing the manuscript for printing. I also thank my parents for making my education a priority in their lives. Some quotes from students and ideas in the book emanate from my PhD (1999) thesis and I thank my supervisors, Herb Marsh and Ray Debus, for their support and guidance in this. I would like to extend particular gratitude to Herb Marsh who has been an inspiring and supportive mentor over the past fifteen years. Other student quotes are from a review I conducted for the (Australian) ACT Department of Education, Youth and Family Services and I thank them for funding that review. Thanks also to the many thousands of teachers and students who have participated in my research and professional life and helped me better understand how to build success in the classroom. Many of these students' voices are reported in this book; however, their names and some details have been adjusted to ensure anonymity. Final recognition goes to the many researchers (particularly Martin Covington) whose research and writing have informed my thinking on the ideas and issues I tackle in this book.

Foreword

This book presents an achievement motivation perspective on success, failure and fear in the classroom. It deals with factors and processes relevant to self-esteem, motivation, engagement, self-regulation, control, courage, optimism, pessimism, competition, helplessness, avoidance and teacher–student relationships. These are very powerful factors and processes in students' academic lives. Hence, the ideas and strategies in the book are substantial approaches for building students' success and eliminating students' academic fear and failure.

Alongside the advice presented here it is also important to recognize and respond to other factors affecting students' success, failure and fear. These include (but are not limited to) attention and/or hyperactivity deficits (e.g. ADD/ADHD), Asperger's Syndrome, dyspraxia, dyslexia, dyscalculia, auditory processing difficulties, depression, anxiety and other conditions that impede learning and achievement.

Importantly, it is common for achievement motivation difficulties to stem from these clinical conditions; that is, students who experience these clinical conditions also have difficulty succeeding in class and are also more likely to experience academic failure and fear in the classroom. Hence, it is important to not only address the clinical condition but also the achievement motivation dynamics that have become a problem as well. This book, then, is a companion resource to be used alongside other resources aimed at directly addressing various clinical conditions. Having said this, there are many 'mainstream' students who do not have problematic clinical or learning difficulties but who develop problematic achievement motivation dynamics. Indeed, high ability (gifted) students also present unique challenges in achievement motivation. This book is centrally relevant to these students as well.

*To my wife and children
with love and gratitude*

PART I

ACHIEVEMENT EVOLUTION IN THE CLASSROOM

1

ACHIEVEMENT IN THE TWENTY-FIRST CENTURY

Academic fitness and academic survival

In the course of a person's life, the world will undergo substantial change. Those who learn to achieve as the world changes will go from strength to strength. Those who fail to achieve in this changing world will experience ongoing difficulties on many fronts.

The classroom is one of the most important places where students have the opportunity to learn the skills, attributes and characteristics to achieve in a changing world. Teachers that optimally assist students to achieve are the teachers that will best prepare students for success in a changing world. Teachers presiding over fear and failure in the classroom run the risk of limiting students' potential and capacity to thrive in the world.

Advances in psychology and education provide illuminating perspectives on how some students learn to survive and thrive at school while other students experience significant difficulties getting through. For example, when looking at school through a recently proposed evolutionary psychology lens, we see teachers can do a terrific job helping their students become academically 'fit', preparing them for success in a changing and variable world. These teachers nurture individuality and provide opportunities for all students to succeed in many and varied ways. These teachers manage to cultivate classrooms where failure does not destabilize students' progress. When students make mistakes or fail (as they surely will), these teachers are expert at helping students take the lessons to be learnt to then move onwards and upwards. These teachers foster an atmosphere where fear is not the dominant dynamic in the classroom. When fear arises (as it surely will), these teachers are expert at helping students face it with courage, optimism and energy.

The overall effect of approaching teaching and instruction in these ways is to place students on positive trajectories. These teachers have added great value to students' lives. Unfortunately, however, the academic trajectories of students characterized by fear and failure are not so positive. In fact, these students' achievement is at risk of flatlining or declining.

And so it is that achievement gaps between students grow. So it is that some students' achievement trajectories are very healthy whereas other students' achievement trajectories are highly problematic. So it is that some students become academically fit, thriving through academic development, while other students barely survive school, if at all.

This growing gap between students has been referred to as the 'Matthew Effect' that draws on a passage from the bible (Mt. 25:29: 'For unto every one that hath shall be given, and he shall have abundance; but from him that hath not shall be taken away even that which he hath') in which the strong get relatively stronger and the weak get relatively weaker. Some students operate in classrooms under teachers where all the right buttons are pressed and success in its many forms prevails. Quite the opposite is the case for other students who operate in classrooms under teachers where all the wrong buttons are pressed and both fear and failure in their many forms dominate. The cumulative effect of these two contrasting phenomena means that there is a growing divide between the academic haves and have-nots. To diminish and then eliminate the Matthew Effect there needs to be a concerted effort directed to building success and eliminating fear and failure. As this book will demonstrate, building classroom success is achieved through building student success and eliminating student fear and failure.

The challenges ahead

For many nations in the twenty-first century, industry will be reshaped around environmental demands and pressures; medical advancements will extend the human life span; pharmaceutical developments will present new possibilities for human performance and functioning; communications technology will be reshaped around fibre optics and extreme bandwidth; high-level globalized computing networks will accelerate information production and application; new technologies will allow greater access to cultural phenomena; and, expansion of electronic databases and resources will transform education and learning.

For people who are able to achieve through these massive changes, the twenty-first century holds great promise and opportunity. People who fail to achieve through these changes will increasingly fall behind the pack and experience disadvantage and difficulty that systematically cuts them off from any further achievement possibilities.

The term 'achievement evolution' is used here to refer to individuals' capacity to achieve through various circumstances and conditions. Teachers focused on building success maximize students' achievement evolution. Teachers presiding over classroom fear and failure reduce students' achievement evolution.

A closer look at 'achievement evolution'

It is proposed here that students develop, evolve and adapt through frequent success experiences. The more students attain success, the more their academic fitness is enhanced and the greater their chances of survival in school and beyond. Furthermore, the more they attain success, the better they are able to effectively manage the demands and challenges that are characteristic of a changing world.

In the classroom, 'success' includes marks, literacy, numeracy, effort, persistence, engagement, participation, cooperation, help-giving, personal bests (PBs) and the like. Students' achievement evolution occurs through frequent and sustained attainment of some or all of these successes. The more students attain these important successes, the academically fitter they become. The fitter they become on these important dimensions, the greater their capacity to deal with new academic tasks and challenges; that is, the greater their capacity to deal with their changing environment and its changing demands.

On the other hand, the more fear and failure are the norm in students' academic life, the more they risk becoming relatively weaker and shift to a downward spiral that becomes increasingly difficult to break. The consequences of this are well known. For example, chronic underachievement at school is associated with:

- school drop-out
- truancy
- misbehaviour in the classroom
- disengagement
- difficulties with teachers

In terms of non-academic consequences, chronic underachievement is associated with:

- poor mental and physical health
- low salary throughout life
- unemployment
- affiliation with negative peers

Today's success is tomorrow's success

One of the strongest predictors of success is success. On virtually every achievement-relevant measure one cares to consider, there is a very high correlation between prior attainment and subsequent attainment. What is one of the best predictors of one's test result next week? Generally, one's test result this week. What are among the best predictors of students' motivation and engagement down the track? In large part, students' current motivation and engagement. How hard will students try tomorrow? Generally, how hard they are trying today.

Sadly, this holds for fear and failure as well. Failure today risks failure tomorrow, next week and next term. Fear today has a high chance of being played out again and again down the track.

Recent large-scale studies are illustrative. Conducting overarching meta-analyses investigating predictors of student achievement, researchers have demonstrated among the highest effect sizes are related to achievement factors themselves (e.g. prior achievement, ability, work completion, marks). Hence, teachers' efforts to enhance student success and reduce failure down the track must begin today, now.

Students inherit their own success and failure

If today's success and failure have a strong chance of being tomorrow's success and failure, then it follows that students inherit their academic outcomes from one situation to another. If we think of academic life as comprising multiple achievement stages (e.g. primary school to high school; junior high school to middle high school; senior high school to college/university), then students who attain success in one stage and inherit it in another are likely to succeed in that subsequent life stage. For example, a student who succeeds in senior high school and inherits that success (and the attributes that caused it) at university, is more likely to succeed at university.

On the other hand, students who do not attain success in an earlier academic stage are not well placed to succeed in a subsequent academic stage. For example, a student who 'fails' in junior high school, and who moves into middle high school without developing the important attributes needed to succeed, will inherit a poor skill set and track record that increase the chances of continued 'failure'.

In sum, for students to succeed through the academic lifespan, it is important that they inherit success and skills from one academic stage to another. Students who inherit the success and skills required to achieve in new and challenging achievement settings will demonstrate more positive achievement trajectories than those who do not. Students who inherit fear and failure from one achievement setting to another will demonstrate weaker achievement trajectories. Hence, promoting success for students, while at the same time reducing fear and failure, are the building blocks for achievement and achievement evolution.

In what ways can students succeed?

Because success is the core element of achievement evolution, it follows that greater access to success will better position students to evolve in the classroom academically and become academically stronger. If this is the case, then it also follows that expanding the range and diversity of success experiences expands students' potential for achievement evolution. Because tomorrow's achievement evolution is very much a function of today's success, a greater diversity of available success experiences has the potential to support students' achievement evolution. Hence, the availability of diverse success experiences is important for students to get ahead in school.

Over the past four decades, various researchers have looked at the many ways students can succeed in the classroom. My own research has suggested two frameworks for capturing the diverse ways students can succeed. One framework looks at success in terms of 'product' and 'process' outcomes.

Process outcomes include factors such as:

- effort
- engagement
- skill development
- participation
- attendance
- self-concept
- persistence
- enjoyment of school

Product outcomes include factors such as:

- achievement
- attainment
- performance
- rank
- marks

Another framework I have developed addresses the multiple dimensions of academic motivation and engagement. Contextualizing motivation and engagement in a multidimensional way communicates to students that there are many ways in which they can succeed from a motivation and engagement perspective. I have proposed the Motivation and Engagement Wheel as an integrative way to represent these different parts of motivation and engagement. It separates these different parts into positive thoughts, positive behaviours, negative thoughts and negative behaviours. The Wheel is presented in the diagram below.

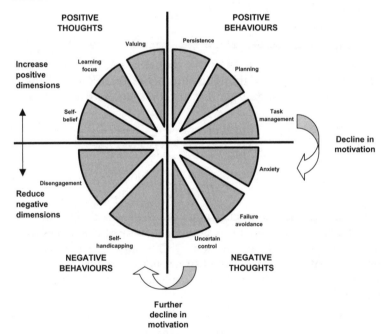

Note: The Motivation and Engagement Wheel reproduced with permission from Martin, A. (2003). '*How to Motivate your Child for School and Beyond*'. Sydney: Bantam and Lifelong Achievement Group (www.lifelongachievement.com).

Positive thoughts include:

- self-belief
- valuing school
- learning focus

Positive behaviours include:

- planning
- task management
- persistence

Negative thoughts include:

- anxiety
- failure avoidance
- uncertain control

Negative behaviours include:

- self-handicapping
- disengagement

From a motivation and engagement perspective, students can succeed by increasing the positive thoughts and behaviours and reducing the negative thoughts and behaviours. Each of these key motivation and engagement factors is summarized below.

POSITIVE THOUGHTS – STUDENTS SUCCEED BY *INCREASING*...

Self-belief

Self-belief is students' belief and confidence in their ability to understand or to do well in schoolwork, to meet challenges they face, and to perform to the best of their ability. Students who have a positive self-belief tend to get better results, do difficult schoolwork confidently, feel optimistic, try hard and enjoy school.

Valuing school

Valuing school is how much students believe what they learn at school is useful, important and relevant to them or to the world in general. If students value school, they tend to be interested in what they learn, persist when schoolwork gets difficult, and enjoy school.

Learning focus

Students who are learning-focused are interested in developing new skills, improvement, PBs, understanding new things, and doing a good job for its own sake and not just for rewards. They are less focused on comparing themselves with others, working only for marks, or how others see them. The more students are learning-focused, the more they enjoy their schoolwork, the less anxious they feel, and the more they can give good quality attention to the task at hand.

POSITIVE BEHAVIOURS – STUDENTS SUCCEED BY *INCREASING*...
Persistence

School involves difficult and challenging schoolwork. To effectively deal with the challenges, students need a level of persistence that can get them through. Persistence is what can make the difference between students who get stuck academically and students who push through to succeed. Persistence is what helps students be solution-focused and encourages them to deal with difficult situations in new and better ways.

Planning

Planning is how much students plan assignments, homework and study, and how much they keep track of their progress. If students plan and monitor schoolwork, they tend to feel in control of schoolwork, persist at challenging schoolwork, and make good use of their time and abilities.

Task management

Task management is the way students use study time, organize a study timetable, and choose and arrange where they study or do homework. If students effectively manage study, they tend to study in places that maximize concentration, use study time well, and plan and stick to a study or homework timetable.

11

NEGATIVE THOUGHTS – STUDENTS SUCCEED BY *REDUCING*...

Uncertain control

Students uncertain in control believe there is little or nothing they can do to avoid failure or to repeat or attain success. Students have a sense of control when they are clear about how to do well or how to avoid doing poorly. Students who have a strong sense of control believe they can influence outcomes in their school life. For example, they believe that through appropriate quality and quantity of effort they can avoid failure or attain success.

Anxiety

Anxiety has two parts: feeling nervous and worrying. Feeling nervous is the uneasy or sick feeling students get when they think about or do their schoolwork, assignments or exams. Worrying is their fear about not doing very well in their schoolwork, assignments or exams. If students are too anxious, they tend to have difficulty concentrating, paying attention, remembering things and doing good quality schoolwork. In terms of school, test anxiety is the most common type of anxiety that students experience.

Failure avoidance

Students are failure-avoidant when the main reason they do their schoolwork is to avoid doing poorly or to avoid being seen to do poorly. If students are failure-avoidant, they tend to fear failure, feel pessimistic, and feel anxious when thinking about or doing their schoolwork.

NEGATIVE BEHAVIOURS – STUDENTS SUCCEED BY *REDUCING*...

Self-handicapping

Students self-handicap when they do things that reduce their success at school. Examples are putting off doing an assignment or wasting time while they are meant to be studying for an exam.

If students self-handicap, they do not feel so good about being at school and tend not to achieve as highly as they are able.

Disengagement

Disengagement refers to thoughts and feelings of giving up, trying less and less each week, detachment from school and schoolwork, feelings of helplessness, and little or no involvement in class or school activities.

I have also developed the Motivation and Engagement Scale (MES) that assesses students on each part of the Wheel. There is a primary/elementary school version of the MES, a high school version, and a university/college version. Teachers, counsellors and psychologists can use the MES to identify students' motivation and engagement strengths (successes) and also to identify what factors may need to be addressed to improve students' achievement evolution. The MES is accessed via Lifelong Achievement Group (www.lifelongachievement.com). There is also an accompanying Motivation and Engagement Workbook, a self-paced program for students to sustain motivation strengths and improve motivation weaknesses. The Workbook is also available via Lifelong Achievement Group (www.lifelongachievement.com).

Obviously the Wheel and process/product success factors are not the only ways to succeed – there are many other ways to attain success in the classroom. The point of the Wheel and the process/product framework is to demonstrate the multiple dimensions teachers can open up as possible successes in students' academic lives. If students define success too narrowly (e.g. only in terms of rank or marks), then they limit their access to success. Because today's success is fundamental to success down the track, it is important to build into classroom life as many genuine success opportunities as possible.

These approaches to diverse success experiences are just some of the ways in which educational and psychological research has shown that it is possible to characterize success and competence from diverse and multidimensional perspectives. When a greater range of success is recognized and nurtured by teachers, more students have greater access to success. In so doing, achievement evolution is possible for a greater number of students and the classrooms to which they belong.

In what ways can students 'fail'?

To the extent that there are many ways students can succeed, there are also many ways they can 'fail'. For example, the process and product outcomes described above can be turned on their head to reflect a pattern of failure.

Process 'failures' include factors such as:

- not trying
- disengagement
- deterioration of skill
- school refusal or drop-out
- negative self-concept
- giving up on tasks
- unhappiness at school

Product 'failures' include factors such as:

- underachievement
- low attainment
- poor performance
- low rank
- unsatisfactory marks

As is the case with success, because today's failure is predictive of failure down the track, it is important to address the many ways failure can play out in the classroom. Hence, building student success is not just about maximizing achievement and competence; it is also about effectively tackling failure (and other problematic factors such as fear) in its many forms.

Conclusion

This book is about success, failure and fear in the classroom. Promoting success and eliminating fear and failure are pivotal to students' achievement and their capacity to achieve well beyond their school years. The attributes and characteristics instilled in students as teachers build student success will also be fundamental to students' capacity to achieve in a changing world. Teachers substantially contribute to students' achievement evolution through school, students' academic fitness, and students' capacity to recognize and seize the opportunities ahead of them in the twenty-first century.

From here this book is organized into three further sections:

- Part 2: Success in the classroom
- Part 3: Fear and failure in the classroom
- Part 4: Building classroom success, eliminating academic fear and failure

Together, these sections and their component chapters unpack the core dynamics that constitute the fabric of achievement, motivation, and engagement – and the many positive approaches teachers can employ to promote students' success and achievement trajectories.

PART 2
SUCCESS IN THE CLASSROOM

2

SUCCESS SEEKERS

As a result of effective pedagogy, what do we want from students? If teachers have a substantial impact on students' academic trajectories (and they do), what motivation and achievement styles are the best to cultivate in the classroom?

In guiding an answer to these questions it is useful to consider attributes that we might want to foster in the classroom and attributes that we might want to minimize or eliminate.

Factors we might want to foster include:

- optimism
- energy
- effort
- hope
- resilience
- confidence
- persistence

Factors we would seek to minimize or eliminate include:

- fear
- doubt
- pessimism
- helplessness
- negativity
- avoidance

It turns out that attributes and characteristics in the first list reflect what researchers call 'success seeking' or 'success striving' styles. Attributes in the second list reflect 'fear of failure', 'failure avoidance', 'success avoidance' and 'failure acceptance' styles. This book is about promoting success styles and reducing fear and failure styles.

Some of the key features of success seekers are as follows:

- forward-looking with optimism, not pessimism
- resilient, not bluffed by setback
- step up to challenge, not shrink from it
- enjoy school and schoolwork
- see school (and childhood/youth) as a journey more than a race
- broad definitions of what 'success' means
- quietly confident, not arrogant or defensive

Graham, age 15, has just started senior high school. These are the final two years and every assessment and exam counts towards the end-of-school result. On top of this, the work has just got a whole lot more difficult. Whereas many of his friends are showing signs of shakiness, uncertainty and fear in the face of these new pressures, Graham is travelling well. He is not finding it easy, but he is not overwhelmed in the ways others are. The reason for this essentially comes down to his mindset – a mindset that has been developing through junior and middle high school, predominantly cultivated at home and by one particularly influential teacher. This mindset has Graham very focused on doing better than he has done before (not focused on doing better than other students), taking on board his teachers' feedback, seeing this feedback as information about the task and his schoolwork (not information about him as a person or his future potential), and looking forward with optimism (not with fear or pessimism). This mindset underpins Graham's academic resilience and is the fuel for his positive academic trajectory through these final and challenging years of school.

Reflecting all these positive attributes, Graham is a success seeker. These (and other) attributes are the focus of this chapter.

Forward-looking

Students who are success seekers are forward-looking, constantly asking themselves: How can I improve? How can I get ahead? How can I master this material? How can I become more competent? How can I learn more effectively? How can I develop my skills further?

Having these questions drive their effort and energy means they are oriented to personal potential, personal improvement, personal excellence and PBs. In contrast, students focused on fear and failure tend to be backward-looking, dwelling on past poor performance or 'near misses'. If they are forward-looking, it is usually with pessimism, fear and foreboding.

Students who are success seekers are not bluffed by setback, poor performance, failure or academic adversity. They take the lesson to be learnt and move on. They do not dwell on the mistake; they learn from it. They do not conclude they are dumb or no good; they see mistakes and setbacks as reflecting on their effort, attitude, or the way they went about the task, which can all be improved next time. They do not assume that past failure will predict future failure. They do not let setback turn into self-doubt and so stay resilient in the face of setback. They keep negative outcomes in perspective and do not make mountains out of molehills.

Pursuit of challenge

Success seekers are not always succeeding. They do hit adversity and setback at school, but it is their response to this adversity that distinguishes them as success seekers. They learn from setback and get on with their lives, looking to implement their newly learnt lesson at the next opportunity.

Because 'failure' does not have the sting for success seekers that it does for other students, success seekers do not live in fear of failure. This being the case, they are prepared to take on challenges that might present some risk of failure but also the chance to extend them. This is how they maintain a positive trajectory over time. Graham, for example, reports great satisfaction in 'just doing or knowing something that you've never done before and getting the hang of it'. By tackling challenges on a regular basis, success seekers are constantly engaged in opportunities to improve and develop. Certainly, some challenges will not pay off, but over time, most of them will.

This leads to another important point: success seekers take on appropriate challenges. They do not take on challenges that are below their capacity and that will not extend them. They do not take on challenges that are too ahead of them and that guarantee failure. Instead, they take on a challenge that is a touch ahead of where they are at. This maximizes the chances of success (but does not guarantee it) and moves them ahead at the same time. Their development, then, is a constant pursuit of challenge that moves them ahead bit by bit. As Graham commented, 'If it's not a challenge it's not really learning, you're just learning the same thing over and over again'.

School/life balance

Success seekers also tend to have balance in their lives. They are not the perfectionists (discussed later) driven by fear to such an extent that they have no down time, no Saturday sport, little time with friends, or little time reading for pleasure or playing electronic games. The success seekers do some of these, and as a consequence do not sacrifice all their precious childhood to academic results. They get the balance right: Working hard at school and schoolwork, and allowing some time to recharge and smell the roses.

Success seekers enjoy school – why wouldn't they? School is not steeped in fear. Failure is not salient in their minds. They are not dwelling on past potholes. They are not looking ahead with dread or foreboding. They are not high in self-doubt; rather, success and competence are more a priority. Learning, skill development, understanding and solving problems are foremost in their minds. When these positive foci are the bases of one's academic life, the stage is set for enjoyment and satisfaction at school and in schoolwork.

School as a journey, not a race

Students who reflect a success-seeking profile tend to see school (and childhood) as a journey more than a race. The use of the term 'success seeking' is not to imply that they are driven to win. In fact, they are more focused on their own progress than focused on beating other students. They are not constantly measuring themselves up against others, making judgements about themselves on the basis of how they compare, or monitoring other students' progress. They do not ask other students what mark they got for this or that. If, on occasion, they do look at other students' performance, it is so they can learn how to do things better.

Because success seekers tend to see school as a journey more than a race, their definition of 'success' tends to be quite broad. While recognizing that marks are important, 'success' for them also encompasses things such as effort, cooperation, class participation, learning new things, seeing a new way of doing something, understanding two points of view, personal progress, help-giving and more. Importantly, all these things factor into their self-esteem. By implication, their self-esteem is not

23

excessively dependent on any one thing. Perhaps most importantly, it is not excessively dependent on their academic results.

The effect of all this is to have a broadly based self-esteem that
is not threatened by 'failure' in a particular area, but resilient and
ready to bounce back from 'failure' if it should occur. Amanda,
age 18, for example, reported that incompetence was not a threat
to her feelings about herself. According to her, 'I'd probably be
cross with myself, but I don't think I was less of a person for it'.
Amanda goes on, 'If I can grasp something by stretching my
mind or worked really hard on something then I've made
progression in myself and I'm proud of myself, more so than
being able to do something better than someone else'.

Quiet confidence and personal excellence

Success seekers are not arrogant, vocal or demonstrative in their
pursuits. In fact, these characteristics often reflect defensiveness
underpinned by fear. Students who need to demonstrate
superiority, are overly public about their success, or present
themselves as superior to other students can be the ones most
unsure of themselves, most in need of approval, and in greatest
fear of disapproval.

Instead, because the success seeker is motivated by personal
excellence and personal potential, this is exactly how it stays –
personal. They do not shrink from public accolade, but they do
not make more of it than is appropriate and they do not pursue
it. They set their own goals and quietly strive to meet them.
When goals are met, they are satisfied, accept praise from others,
and then move on. According to Joan, age 16, 'It's sort of an
inside personal thing'.

Achieving to please themselves, not others

Following from the above point about personal excellence,
success seekers are also more interested in achieving to please
and satisfy themselves more than pleasing and satisfying others.
As Lucy, age 17, noted, 'You've got to do it for yourself'.

There are risks in being motivated to please others. One is that
it is impossible to please others all the time, inevitably leading to
disappointment and 'failure'. Another is that students never
come to know themselves and this can lead to ineffective

decisions about school subjects, careers and the like; that is, always trying to please others and shaping attitudes and behaviours around others does not allow students to define their own lives. Another is that there tends to be an anxiety in the lives of students who strive to please others more than themselves. Yet another is that there is less inclination to ask for help because this will risk others suspecting or doubting the student's ability.

Success seekers are free of these pressures. For example, as Martina, age 16, approached the end of the year and needed to consult teachers in preparation for exams, she reported 'I'm getting close to the end and I think, 'Stuff it, if I don't ask now, I'm never going to know'', reflecting a greater interest in learning from others than how she is seen by others. Cathy, age 17, was similar, 'I'm not worried about approaching the teacher. I'm not worried about them thinking, "This girl's stupid"'.

Stars in their own right

As indicated above, do not assume success seekers are necessarily the top performers. As discussed later in this book, some top performers are driven by fear and there is a price to pay for this. Some success seekers may be in the middle of the pack from an achievement perspective. Importantly, however, if they are working to potential, forward-looking, not bluffed by setback, and staying buoyant through school, then they can be considered highly successful from a motivation, engagement and personal potential perspective. Hence, even though they might not be the top in marks, they can be considered successful from many other important perspectives.

Too often students labour under the view that the only way to succeed is to be a top performer. Sadly, this can often be perpetuated or fuelled at school and in the home. In fact, it can be fuelled in society as well – school league tables are often published in newspapers and online in some shape or form. Hence, society comes to value academic results above other forms of achievement. However, the more students labour under this narrow view of success, the more they cut themselves off from other success opportunities. Moreover, this narrow view of success means many students never feel successful. The success seeker, on the other hand, has a broader view of what success is and so has greater access to the many success opportunities available in academic life.

Success seekers, then, are able to disentangle themselves from the classic zero-sum game problem at school. This game goes something like this: If success is only defined in terms of rank, then some students will 'succeed' while the rest must 'fail'. As this plays out, school becomes nothing more than a constant sifting of winners and losers. The success seekers free themselves from this potentially deflating cycle. They see success in many ways, and through this have greater access to it. Greater access to success inspires hope, optimism, energy and engagement.

Broader yields of success seeking

Thus far the discussion has centred on the academic merits of success seeking. It is also evident that success seekers operate in effective ways outside their academic lives. They take their positive attributes and inject them into other parts of their personal and interpersonal worlds.

Because success seekers reflect quite positive attributes and are generally upbeat (but in a measured and appropriate way), they are also generally likeable. It is quite pleasant to be around them. Hence, their success-seeking profile has implications in other parts of their lives. Although this book is not about social development, it is important to recognize that characteristics reflected in one's academic life have the potential to facilitate or impede characteristics in other life areas.

Success seekers are also more effective in their interpersonal and emotional lives. For example, they have the courage to ask a girl out for a date and are not crushed if she declines. They do not conclude they lack worth, they do not conclude they are unlovable, and they do not conclude they will be relegated to a lonely life. This sort of response to setback also makes for a stable and resilient emotional life. True, they are disappointed. True, they feel a bit hurt. These are very normal and healthy reactions; indeed, to not experience them is unhealthy. But they do not blow these negative emotions out of proportion and so keep their emotional life in a healthy balance.

Long-term yields of success seeking

It is also important to note that the attributes of success seekers are attributes that underpin success in post-school pathways. Work is a great example. Although each job or profession requires a particular level of ability and educational attainment to gain entry, how do we explain the enormous variability in success within a particular job or profession? Some people fly in their careers while others never go as far as they could.

One major factor concerns individuals' achievement motivation style. Those oriented to success, competence, development and personal excellence tend to cope very well with workplace pressures and demands. They also deal with workplace setback more effectively than others. Because they have learnt to respond to setback in such positive and resilient ways, they are able to regroup and look to implement the lessons learnt in their next project. Further, because working life involves many setbacks over the course of one's adulthood, those who are able to respond best to these setbacks have the most to gain from them. Thus again, the achievement and success gap widens as some people systematically bounce back from setback at work while others are bluffed and impeded by it.

It follows that students who develop success-seeking attributes during their school life are laying the foundations for potential success in their post-school pathways. Although it is never too late to develop these attributes, they are more readily developed in younger life. Schools and teachers who look to foster success seeking in their students' academic lives are investing in these students' lives and future life effectiveness.

How do students come to be success seekers?

There are a few factors that underpin success seeking and which give clues as to how some students come to be success seekers while other students are quite clearly driven by fear and failure.

The first relates to temperament. There are some children who by their basic nature are optimistic and buoyant. There are other children who are more pessimistic by nature. Hence, one part of success seeking is a result of one's temperament and personality. Importantly, however, a child's environment can either sustain or impede this positive temperament. For example, home environments that dwell on fear and failure will significantly diminish a child's success orientation. Similarly, a classroom where fear prevails will negatively impact a success seeker's positive disposition. Thus, educators and the home have an important part to play in sustaining success seekers' positive way of going about things. As one student observed, 'Good teachers can make any subject good. But even if it's your favourite subject, a bad teacher can make you lose confidence in yourself and you don't do well'.

This leads to another factor underpinning success seeking: environment. Over and above a child's temperament it is possible to sustain success seeking in success seekers and to build success seeking in students for whom fear and failure may be more of a focus. For some students this will simply mean encouraging them to have different reasons for doing their schoolwork; for example, working to improve rather than working to avoid failure or working to learn rather than working to avoid looking dumb. For other students, it will mean a systemic campaign to reduce failure in their academic life. This is discussed in detail in later chapters.

Students can also learn success seeking from significant others modelling successful behaviours and attitudes. Watching parents behave in optimistic and empowered ways is good modeling for success seeking. Seeing parents learn and bounce back from mistakes is good modelling for success seeking. Noticing parents take on challenge with courage and hope is good modelling for success seeking. Indeed, these can be modelled in the classroom as well. Every school day and every school hour, students watch teachers react to and respond to challenge and setback. They also observe teachers' general disposition to academic subject matter and school life – is it oriented to optimism and confidence or pessimism and self-doubt?

Peers also have an influence. Mixing with friends who are positively oriented to school and schoolwork can be helpful. In fact, research into extra-curricular activity suggests its positive effects are partly due to the fact that it has children mixing with positive peers. Positive peer affiliation has two effects. The first is that it helps develop positive attitudes and behaviours towards positive things (e.g. school). The second is that it reduces or eliminates exposure to negative attitudes and behaviours: a child cannot be playing a game of football or basketball at the same time as hanging around the shopping mall getting into trouble.

As Graham commented, 'One group will just say school sucks and life sucks. They just come to school, go to lunch and have a smoke or something. I try to avoid them'. Another student noted, 'Say your friends have the same teacher as you and you don't like that teacher. They can put that teacher in a new light and make you see that they're okay, that they might be a good teacher'.

The barriers to success seeking

As success seeking is being promoted in the classroom, it will also be necessary to ensure that problematic motivation and achievement styles are dealt with. These represent barriers that can undermine success seeking. Two major barriers along these lines are fear and failure. Interestingly, fear and failure as stand-alone factors are not actually the problem. The problem is (a) the meaning students attach to fear and failure and (b) the ways they deal with and respond to fear and failure.

Some students attach negative meaning to fear and failure – seeing nothing to learn from them and everything to lose from them. Some students respond to fear and failure with avoidance and helplessness. Some students respond to fear and failure with obsessive effort at the expense of other important life tasks and activities in childhood and youth. Examples of these problematic orientations to fear and failure include:

- perfectionism
- defensive pessimism
- defensive optimism
- self-handicapping
- disengagement
- success avoidance

Because these are such major barriers to success and success seeking, I deal with them in detail in the next chapters.

In contrast, some students attach a constructive meaning to fear and failure – seeing something to learn from them. Some students respond to fear and failure with courage. Some students respond to fear and failure with high levels of effort and energy, keeping things in perspective and moving forward. These students are the success seekers.

Conclusion

There are two fundamental pathways in a classroom: one oriented to success, engagement, motivation and optimism; and one oriented to and driven by fear and failure. The former path is referred to as success seeking and has been the focus of this chapter. Success seekers are forward-looking, focused on mastery and competence, not bluffed by setback, oriented to personal excellence and personal potential, and not dominated or motivated by fear and self-doubt.

Success seeking is a result of numerous factors. Temperament and personality play a role. For example, some students are naturally optimistic. Environment also has an effect. For example, the benefits of home and school promoting success seeking are evident. In fact, negative environments can seriously challenge the optimism of students who are naturally optimistic. Importantly, however, positive environments can also build success seeking into students who tend to be pessimistic by nature.

Building student and classroom success is done in two ways: (a) promoting success, optimism and competence; and (b) reducing fear and failure. Having looked at success, optimism and competence in this chapter, the next few chapters look closely at fear and failure.

PART 3

FEAR AND FAILURE IN THE CLASSROOM

3

FEAR, FAILURE AND SELF-ESTEEM

School has the potential to be a major source of personal and academic fulfilment. However, the reality is that fear and failure pervade one, some or all school subjects for most students at some point in their academic lives. Rather than respond to fear and failure in courageous and constructive ways, many of these students engage in quite self-defeating behaviour in a bid to salvage some self-worth from an otherwise dispiriting situation.

This section examines the ways fear and failure play out in students' academic lives and the counterproductive strategies students use in response to this fear and failure. It also examines the successful strategies educators can put in place to reduce fear and failure in the classroom and the tactics they can use to help students respond to these problematic outcomes in more positive and productive ways.

Classroom audit

Many teachers underestimate the extent to which fear and failure characterize students in their classroom. This is because fear and failure play out in many different and surreptitious ways. Consider the following questions:

- To what extent do your students jeopardize their chances of success by doing anything but working on the task at hand (e.g. procrastinating)?
- To what extent do your students think they are going to fail or perform poorly even though they have done well in the past?
- How well do your students cope leading up to high pressure performance situations such as exams?
- To what extent do your students set expectations that are too easy or too hard to reach?
- To what extent do your students tackle tasks that are clearly too easy or clearly too difficult?
- To what extent do your students shrink from academic challenges?
- How well do your students bounce back from a poor performance?
- To what extent do your students give up too easily – sometimes not even try?
- How many students in your class have disengaged from school and schoolwork?

These questions refer to the different ways students behave when trying to protect their self-esteem in the face of possible failure or poor performance. Failure can be very damaging to students' self-esteem. Because of this, students live in fear of failure and have developed a number of strategies to deal with it. Unfortunately, these strategies are ultimately self-defeating because they increasingly cut students off from success and success opportunities.

Importantly, these self-defeating strategies are not the only ways students can respond to their fear of failure or poor performance. There are many positive ways to deal with this fear that can maximize students' chances of success. There are, then, ways students can eliminate fear from their academic lives and learn more effective strategies to deal with the possibility of failure. By eliminating such fear from their lives, students become motivated to strive for success. Being success-focused makes for a much happier and satisfying academic life.

The fear and failure process

Students' behaviour in the academic context is often based on their need to avoid failure and protect their self-esteem. Self-esteem refers to the extent to which students feel good about themselves and feel valued by others. Protecting self-esteem is one of students' highest priorities. Students strive to feel valued and affirmed by themselves and others. They go to great lengths to avoid disapproval – sometimes at great academic cost to themselves.

Another important idea to understand is that much of students' self-esteem tends to be based on cleverness and competence. They feel a higher level of self-esteem when they demonstrate cleverness and competence. They feel a lower level of self-esteem when their cleverness and competence are in question. This is because many students link their worth to cleverness and success. This is illustrated in the following diagram.

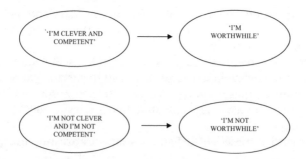

The link students make between their cleverness and their worth is critical because it is this that makes them vulnerable when there is a risk that they might fail. If students fail, they may think they are not clever or competent. If they think they are not clever or competent there is a risk that they lack feelings of self-worth. This is illustrated in the following diagram.

The final problematic link students make is between how worthwhile they feel and their self-esteem. Essentially, when students do not feel worthwhile, their self-esteem suffers. The following diagram presents the full process of how failure leads to low self-esteem.

Students' responses to their fear of failure

What do students do when they are faced with the possibility of failure and the damage to their self-esteem that this may cause? Too many students come to learn that the best way they can avoid feelings of poor self-esteem is to engage in some form of self-esteem defence. Unfortunately, the way they often do this is through problematic self-defeating behaviour.

As will be seen in the following chapters, what these self-defeating strategies ensure is failure with dignity. By failure with dignity, students' failure or poor performance are not seen to be because they are not clever or competent (which leads to low self-esteem). Rather, failure or poor performance are seen to be results of some other factor that cannot be linked to students' possible incompetence. By redirecting failure or poor performance away from their lack of cleverness or competence, students manage to protect their self-esteem.

Take the case of Rebecca, age 14, who has an exam on Friday and is terrified that she will fail it. Rather than study hard the night before to maximize her chances of success, she goes to a party. Sure enough, she does fail the exam. Importantly, however, she tells herself and others that she failed because she went partying. By implication, she cannot be accused of failing because she is not clever. In fact, she has managed to fail with her dignity and self-esteem intact; that is, she has redirected the failure away from a possible lack of cleverness and onto the party. All we can say about her is, 'She shouldn't have gone partying on Thursday night', and not, 'She mustn't be very smart'. Now that her cleverness is not under threat, neither is her self-esteem. She has, then, defended her self-esteem through self-defeating protective behaviour.

What about John, age 14, a member of the school swimming team who does not train leading up to an important swimming competition? He finds all sorts of excuses for not training – on one day it is too hot, on another day his back hurts, and on another day he just cannot organize himself to get to the pool. If he performs poorly in the competition, he can deflect the cause of that poor performance away from a possible lack of competence and onto the fact that he did not train. The worst we can say about him is, 'He really should have trained before the competition', and not, 'He mustn't be a very good swimmer'. John has manoeuvred so that he cannot be said to be incompetent. Now that his competence is not under threat, neither is his self-esteem. John has defended his self-esteem through self-defeating protective behaviour.

As students use these problematic strategies on an increasing basis, they not only result in consistent failure or poor performance and feelings of helplessness, but they start to lose their protective value. For example, if John consistently failed to train and consistently performed poorly in competition, we would begin to suspect John's motives for not training. No doubt John would also be refused entry to subsequent competitions. We would probably come to a conclusion that John was covering up something worse than what is probably the case. For example, we may think that John was more incompetent than he actually is. Most importantly, however, John sets himself on an ever downwardly spiralling cycle of poor performance that becomes increasingly difficult to break. Hence, his self-protection leads to a downward spiralling of both performance and self-esteem. While at first enticing, self-defeating protective behaviour eventually proves to be quite a problematic path to tread.

Rebecca and John have elected to engage in failure-oriented behaviour rather than strive for success. They could have elected to strive for success by trying hard. One of the most important messages in this book is that students can attain success when they try, practise and commit to the challenges before them. Unfortunately, however, there are barriers that prevent students from wanting to try hard and this book is also about showing how to break down those barriers.

The varieties of failure-oriented behaviours

There are many failure-oriented strategies students use to defend their self-esteem. Students are quite inventive creatures and have at their disposal a variety of tricks, twists and strategies to defend themselves in the face of possible failure or poor performance. Each of these varies in the degree to which they are self-defeating and problematic. Some are quite clearly and immediately acts of self-defeat. Others make students vulnerable to failure further down the track and so are self-defeating in the longer term. The following self-defeating behaviours are dealt with in this book:

- self-handicapping
- defensive pessimism
- defensive optimism
- overstriving and perfectionism

- success avoidance
- learnt helplessness

Self-handicapping

Self-handicapping is a flagship self-protection strategy (see Chapter 5). Students self-handicap by putting obstacles in their path to success and then using these obstacles as the excuse if they perform poorly. In the examples above, both Rebecca and John were self-handicappers. The obstacles set up by Rebecca were a lack of study and a hangover. The obstacle set up by John was a lack of training. What does this achieve? It is shown throughout this book that when self-handicappers do not do so well, they can blame the obstacle and not a possible lack of competence.

Many self-handicapping tactics are discussed in this book. These range from behaviours that most students are guilty of such as procrastination to more extreme behaviours involving the use of alcohol or other drugs. By redirecting their failures or poor performances away from their lack of cleverness or competence and onto the procrastination or the alcohol, students protect their self-esteem. Self-handicapping is self-defeating because students actively limit their chances of possible success.

Defensive pessimism

Students can be quite strategic about the expectations they set for themselves. Defensive pessimism is where students set unreaslitically low expectations leading up to a performance or evaluation situation.

> Toby, age 14, is a pessimist when it comes to his academic achievement. Every exam period, he is pessimistic about how he will do. This has a number of advantages. For a start, he has set a lower standard that is easier to reach (he has lowered the bar, so to speak) – so failure is less likely. Second, by being pessimistic, he cushions himself from the blow of failure if it should occur – that is, he has prepared himself for poor results so that they are not so hard-hitting.

Defensive pessimism, then, is a way students can reduce the likelihood of failing or at least prepare themselves for the disappointment if they do. It is, therefore, a self-protective strategy of choice for many students. Defensive pessimism is self-defeating behaviour because it puts the focus on one's short-comings and negative outcomes and sets standards that do not challenge or extend them (see Chapter 6).

Defensive optimism

Students sometimes hold expectations that are way too high – this is called defensive optimism. This almost guarantees failure because the high expectations are near impossible to reach. While this can guarantee failure, it ensures failure with some dignity – the failure is seen to be because of unrealistically high expectations (anyone would have failed against those expectations!) and not because one is incompetent. By deflecting the cause of failure or poor performance away from possible incompetence and onto unrealistically high expectations, students' self-esteem remains intact – for the time being at least.

> Take the example of Joshua, age 17, a student of average ability, who told everyone he was going to study Law at the best university but who failed to get the grades required. We are just as likely to think that Joshua set unrealistically high expectations as we are to think that he was not clever enough to qualify. Thus, Joshua has altered the meaning of his failure so that it reflects as much on his expectations as it does on his cleverness. By minimizing the extent to which we think poorly of his competence or cleverness, he has minimized the damage to his self-esteem.

Defensive optimism is self-defeating behaviour because the unrealistically high expectations increase the chances of failure or poor performance (see Chapter 6).

Overstriving (and perfectionism)

Of course, many students deal with their fear and failure by succeeding. These students are referred to as overstrivers (or perfectionists) (see Chapter 8). Overstrivers fear failure or poor performance intensely but deal with this fear by doing their absolute most to succeed. Overstriving is self-protection because it protects students from failure by guaranteeing success. Over-strivers strive for success because they are fearful of failure or poor performance. Thus, they share a very similar motivation to the other failure fearers described above. They are different, however, because they actually invest vast amounts of study and effort.

One may wonder why overstriving is a problem if it usually leads to success. It can be a problem because overstrivers do not deal with poor performance very well: following poor perfor-mance, they can take more drastic self-protective action. It is also problematic because overstrivers tend not to enjoy school so much.

Take Bronwyn, age 15, a high ability History student, who works extremely hard at school. She is at pains to write impeccable essays, submits them on time, and even takes herself to extra classes put on by the teacher. However, underpinning all this hard work and motivation is self-doubt and a rather substantial fear of failure. Thus, she does not work hard with the aim to succeed; rather, she works hard to avoid failure or poor performance. This is fine – while she continues to perform well. However, negative feedback from her teacher or a poor mark unsettle her enormously. This is because they confirm her self-doubt. If she receives any more negative feedback, there is an increased possibility she may seek more problematic ways to deal with her fear of failure.

Success avoidance

Fear and failure can also underpin students' motivation to avoid success (see Chapter 9). Success avoidance is where students are fearful of success and try to avoid it. That is, they look to perform more poorly than what they are capable of. There are three types of success avoider.

The first type of success avoider does not want to do well because they will stand out from the crowd or look different from the others. Their thinking goes something like this: 'The nail that sticks out gets hammered – so don't stick out and you won't get hammered'. The failure these students fear is social failure. The second type of success avoider does not want to do well because they will hurt friends and disrupt the rules of the group that dictate a particular level of performance. Again, social failure is the failure these students fear. The third type of success avoider is the student who does not want to do well because then there is more pressure on them to do well next time. The fear these students experience is a fear of future academic failure. All three cases reflect self-defeating behaviour because they reduce students' chances of success in a bid to protect self-esteem – be it social self-esteem or academic self-esteem.

Learned helplessness

One of the most self-defeating protection strategies is to give up trying completely. When students experience repeated failure or poor performance and see no way of avoiding failure in the future, they give up. That is, they learn to be helpless (see Chapter 7).

> Sam, age 14, is a typical example. He has had a bad run on the debating team. It seems that no matter what he does or how he approaches the debate, he performs poorly. He gets it in his head that there is nothing he can do to bounce back. He has become helpless and gives up participating in debates. In fact, even if a teacher tried to convince him he could break the cycle, there is a strong possibility that Sam would not try to turn things around because of his conviction that there is nothing he can do to perform well. Thus, even if the chances of succeeding were to improve, because of his experience of repeated failure and his feelings of helplessness, Sam still does not try.

Learned helplessness can be self-protective in that students do not put their cleverness or competence on the line to be judged. Hence, failure or poor performance in these tasks is because they do not try and not because they are incompetent. Learnt helplessness can be a way to avoid complete damage to one's self-esteem. Learnt helplessness is the ultimate form of self-defeating behaviour in that students give up trying and totally surrender to failure or poor performance.

Summary of failure-oriented strategies

As is clear, a major part of failure-orientation is problematic thinking about oneself and one's schoolwork. The following examples are some of the thinking that marks each of the failure-oriented protective strategies addressed in the following chapters.

- 'If I haven't done much study, then they can't say I'm dumb if I fail' (self-handicapping).
- 'If I set my expectations low, then it's less likely I'll fail against this lower standard' (defensive pessimism).
- 'If I set really high expectations, I can say that anyone would have failed against those expectations' (defensive optimism).
- 'If I work myself to the bone, I won't fail' (overstriving/perfectionism).
- 'If I don't do very well this time, then more won't be expected of me next time' (success avoidance).
- 'I can't fail at something I don't even do' (learned help-lessness/disengagement).

Now compare this failure-oriented thinking profile to the following ways students can think about the challenges before them:

- 'Success is within my reach'.
- 'Every challenge is an opportunity'.
- 'I'm going to work hard to maximize my chances of success'.
- 'I'm going to set realistic but challenging expectations'.
- 'I'm going to choose realistic but challenging tasks to engage in'.
- 'If I succeed once then I can succeed again'.

These thoughts are the hallmarks of success seekers. Importantly, teachers have a big part to play in the extent to which a student is fearful of failure or success-focused. Indeed, this book later outlines 20 Teacher Tips (see Chapter 19) that can be applied in students' lives to help them become success focused and to respond in more courageous and constructive ways to academic fear and failure.

4
SELF-ESTEEM PROTECTION

Before dealing with the numerous forms of fear and failure in detail, it is first important to understand more fully the nature of students' self-esteem protection and the thinking that underpins it. These give us valuable clues in how to eliminate fear and failure in the classroom and form the basis of the Teacher Tips discussed in Chapter 19.

What is self-esteem and why is it important?

Self-esteem is a highly valuable personal asset. Armed with self-esteem, students feel good about their studies and their skills. Armed with self-esteem, students can overcome academic challenges presented to them.

Self-esteem refers to students' feelings of self-acceptance and the extent to which they like and value who they are and what they do. Because the need for self-acceptance is great, students are prepared to go to great lengths to protect themselves when this self-acceptance is threatened.

The following ways that students' positive views about themselves improve them and their performance are:

- Students who think highly of themselves tend to embrace challenging tasks that ultimately improve their skills and enhance their chances of success in future activities and tasks.
- Students who think highly of themselves tend to invest more effort and persistence into tasks.

The following ways that students' negative views about themselves can present problems are:

- Students who think poorly of themselves tend to dwell on their deficiencies and view tasks as more difficult than they really are.
- Students who think poorly of themselves tend to avoid challenging tasks and so cut themselves off from potentially enriching experiences that would otherwise develop them.
- Students who do not think highly of themselves respond to failure with resignation and apathy.
- Students who do not think highly of themselves tend to quickly abandon challenging tasks.

Hence, not only is self-esteem a valuable end in itself, but it also leads to many other benefits that ultimately enhance students' functioning at school. In the case of negative self-esteem, there is an academic price to pay. The questions, then, are: How do students develop a sense of self-esteem? What contributes to students' self-esteem? How is students' self-esteem devalued in the academic context and what threatens it most?

What determines students' self-esteem and why?

Often to their disadvantage, a major factor that determines how students feel about themselves at school is their ability to perform and succeed. This is the case in all arenas – educational, social and sporting. In school it is often the case that students who do well and succeed are seen as more worthy than students who do not. The 'best' students in the school are held in high esteem.

Interestingly, it is not so much the grades they get, the friends they have, or the tournaments they have won that put them in high esteem. Rather, it is the quality underpinning these successes – their competence and cleverness (e.g. academic talent, sporting prowess or social acumen) – that determine worth.

Why do cleverness or competence carry so much weight? Why do we not equate esteem with someone's generosity or the extent to which someone tried hard in a test or a race?

The reason why cleverness and competence are valued above all else is because children come to learn early in life that cleverness and success equate to worth and value – essentially, they receive more approval and affirmation when they demonstrate cleverness or competence. Similarly, early in life children learn that incompetence and failure or poor performance equate to low value and low worth; that is, approval and affirmation are not often forthcoming in the event of failure or poor performance. In this way, the ability to perform becomes directly tied to a person's value and worth. Thus, students learn that failure and poor performance are to be feared because they reflect incompetence and incompetence impacts negatively on worth and self-esteem.

A closer look at how academic achievement determines students' worth and value

As mentioned, early in students' academic lives they learn that academic achievement and their capacity to perform academically bring approval and affirmation. They learn that to be valued and worthwhile, it is best to achieve academically. This is because academic achievement demonstrates competence and cleverness. And so it is through this process that students learn that their worth very much depends on their competence and cleverness.

Home life becomes a breeding ground for the belief that cleverness and competence mean high worth and incompetence means low worth. Many children will hear their parents speak highly of top students in the school. In fact, some parents actually see their children's performance as an indication of their own worth and their children come to learn that their parents value them more highly when they succeed and less highly when they do not.

When children enter school, they are further reminded that cleverness and competence equate with worth. Students come to learn that achievement gains approval and this approval is seen as the mark of a student's worth. Unfortunately, however, in most classrooms where only a few students can get to the top of the pack, this has the effect of communicating to the majority of other students that they lack competence and this leads many to conclude that they lack worth. Classrooms, then, are another training ground in which students learn that it is cleverness and competence that are highly valued (and not, say, trying hard) and the mark of worth.

In sum, as students move through childhood, through adolescence, and into early adulthood, they increasingly value cleverness and achievement and use these as the bases on which to determine their worth and how they feel about themselves.

Fear of failure or poor performance and failure avoidance

Because failure and poor performance are the clearest evidence of incompetence, it is failure and poor performance that most threaten students' self-esteem. Therefore, if their highest priority is to protect their self-esteem, then failure or poor performance are to be feared and avoided above all else. This motivates them to engage in self-defeating protective behaviour.

Surprisingly, however, it is often the case that their self-defeating protective behaviour guarantees failure or poor performance. How can they possibly protect their self-esteem by engaging in strategies that guarantee failure or poor performance? If we look closely, we will see that what they manage to do is change the nature of that failure or poor performance. For example, even though John the swimmer performed poorly (see Chapter 3), he changed it from a poor performance due to incompetence (which would reflect poorly on his worth and damage his self-esteem) to one that was due to insufficient training – something that is not so damaging to his worth and self-esteem. In other words, John has changed his poor performance from one reflecting incompetence to one reflecting low effort. While he has not avoided poor performance, he has changed the way it is seen.

A focus of this book is to build more positive, courageous and constructive foundations for self-esteem and self-worth in the classroom. When students are characterized by these adaptive attributes, fear and failure take a back seat and the stage is set for building student and classroom success.

Conclusion

Self-esteem impacts on how students feel, how students behave and, indeed, their dignity as human beings. Because of this, one of their highest priorities is to protect it. However, most students do not see their self-esteem as a given. Rather, they have learnt that their self-esteem is very much a result of their ability to succeed and perform well. The mistake students make in doing this is to connect their self-esteem with their competence. This makes students vulnerable because if they do not perform well, then their self-esteem is under direct threat.

Students therefore come to fear failure and seek to avoid it at all cost. By avoiding failure or poor performance, their self-esteem is not under threat. However, under many circumstances they cannot avoid failure or poor performance. In such cases they have learnt how to change the meaning of failure or poor performance, or to fail with dignity. For example, they manipulate the amount of effort they put into tasks. By investing less effort, it cannot be concluded that their failure or poor performance are because of incompetence – it is just because they did not try hard enough. In this way, their cleverness and competence are off the hook, and so is their self-esteem. To build classroom success and eliminate fear and failure, it is vital that students develop healthy and robust bases for self-worth – a need so vital that it is a central focus of this book.

5

SELF-HANDICAPPING

I'll keep myself occupied and think, 'I'll do it tomorrow, I'll do it tomorrow,' and then I spend the last week going, 'Oh no!' That happens every single time. No matter how hard I try. I think, 'Okay, I'll start early, I'll go to the library,' but I'm always still up to four o'clock in the morning it's due – every time, no matter what. I've just accepted that it's the way I work. I've been doing it for years. I've always done it. It's not going to change now ... Failure's easier to cope with if you think you haven't put as much work into it.

Carla, age 17

Say an assignment's due on Monday and it's the weekend, I seem to just want to clean. I want to make my room clean, or I just watch TV, or go out. It's just something that happens. You know you've got to do something but you get off track and go somewhere.

Tom, age 16

Self-handicapping occurs when students put obstacles in their path to possible success; that is, they handicap their chances of success. What do they gain by doing this? Well, if they fail or perform poorly, then they can blame the obstacle and not the fact that they may not be clever or competent. As one self-handicapper reported, 'It always helps to have an alibi when I don't do very well'. Because incompetence is not seen to be the cause of their failure or poor performance, they have protected their self-esteem.

Interestingly, if they succeed, then they look even better because they have succeeded in the face of adversity. For example, students who do well in an exam after partying the night before look even brighter than if they had done well after studying hard.

It seems, then, that self-handicappers cannot lose. But this is not the case. As appealing as the possible benefits may appear, it is evident that they are only short-lived and eventually put students in a downward spiral of failure or poor performance from which their self-esteem cannot escape.

Types of self-handicapping

There seem to be countless ways to self-handicap. It is perhaps surprising the lengths to which students go to set up excuses in case they do not do so well. Some of the examples presented below show that self-handicapping can be quite a calculated and deliberate strategy; that is, it is very often thought out beforehand.

Other examples show that students can self-handicap without realizing it. Indeed, there is much debate about the extent to which students are aware of their self-handicapping. Some self-handicappers will quite readily admit to and recognize their self-handicapping while others will not recognize it at all. There will also be some self-handicapping strategies that one student will use but which will not be used by other students. Using one self-handicapping strategy does not mean students necessarily use others. Having said this, the seasoned self-handicapper may have developed quite a collection of self-handicapping strategies and has become skilled at using them at just the right time.

Not trying

One of the most common self-handicapping techniques is to not try. If students fail after not trying, they can blame the fact that they did not try hard enough and not the fact that they might be incompetent. The result is that they protect their self-esteem because their cleverness or competence is not in question. This 'not trying' is self-handicapping because students cut themselves off from success; that is, they handicap their chances of success.

Schools, colleges and universities are fertile territory for this type of self-handicapping. Many students at some stage will have done less study when they were worried about failing or performing poorly. In some ways this might not make sense. Why did they not respond to the possibility of failure or poor performance by trying harder? Surely trying harder would be the best way to avoid failure or poor performance and achieve success.

Unfortunately, it is not this simple. Research has shown that when students fail after trying hard, they are seen to be more incompetent than if they had not tried at all. This is because after trying hard, incompetence is the most likely reason for failure. For some students, trying can be seen as a dangerous thing because if they fail or perform poorly, then they look dumb. On the other hand, if they fail or perform poorly after not trying, then they do not look so dumb. This is because they can blame the failure or poor performance on the fact that they did not try. Because their cleverness or competence is not in question, their self-esteem lives to see another day.

So why should students bother trying at all? Surely, if trying threatens their self-esteem then trying must be a bad thing – and by implication, not trying must be a good way to protect oneself. Unfortunately, not trying will only protect students for so long. After a while, others do not accept the excuse. In fact, they become suspicious. They begin to think that the student is hiding something worse than is really the case. Eventually students' fears actually happen: people think they do not try because they are just not up to the task. Hence, what students have been at such pains to avoid – people thinking they are dumb – happens. Worse still, by this time they have locked themselves into a vicious cycle of poor performance that is difficult to break.

Hence, while not trying is easier and may have a short-term advantage by redirecting the cause of poor performance away from possible incompetence, in the longer term students come unstuck.

Common examples of not trying are:

- not studying enough for exams
- not doing enough work on assignments
- not practising French vocabulary
- not putting enough time into a difficult subject
- not asking for help when it is needed
- not doing enough background research on a project
- not giving some topics proper attention
- not spending enough time on homework
- not preparing for tests

By not trying, students have an excuse if they fail or perform poorly on the exam or assignment. It is because they did not try that these negative outcomes occurred and not because they are incompetent or lack ability. Again, their competence remains intact – for a while – and so does their self-esteem – for a while.

What students do not realize is that they would feel and perform much better in the long run if they tried hard and maximized their chances of success. As they say, nothing succeeds like success, and self-handicappers never give themselves a chance to realize this.

Procrastination

Pointless time wasting? Yeah, I'm the queen of pointless time wasting. I'll say, 'I've got study to do, well I really need to clean my wardrobe, tidy under my bed, clean the fish tank, and visit Grandma'. That way if I don't do so well, I can say I was cleaning my wardrobe or something.

Robin, age 17

Another form of self-handicapping is procrastination. Procrastination is self-handicapping because by putting things off, students are not giving themselves the best chance of succeeding; that is, students are getting in the way of what success would be if they got onto things promptly. Thus, if students fail or perform poorly after having procrastinated, they have an excuse. They can blame their procrastination and not their incompetence. Because their competence is not in question, neither is their self-esteem.

Many students would not agree that their procrastination is a strategy designed to protect their self-esteem. Countless students would simply say, 'I don't know why I procrastinate, it just happens'. Or, 'I'm just lazy, that's all'. However, there is usually a motive for what students do and procrastination is no exception.

Examples of procrastination include:

- putting study off until the last minute
- putting off important tasks at school
- putting off practice or preparation in a particular subject
- putting off asking for help
- putting off the visit to the school psychologist or counsellor
- putting off enrolling in an advanced course
- putting off joining the debating team
- putting off the essay to the following week

For many students, underpinning each of these behaviours is the motive to use the procrastination as the excuse if they fail or perform poorly in some way. Students who fail or perform poorly can blame their procrastination and not their lack of cleverness or competence. People who miss out on the advanced class can blame the fact that they routinely put off important assignments and not their incompetence. Similarly, students who put off asking for help can use that as an excuse if they do not do well.

By putting off the visit to the school psychologist, for example, the student does not have to face up to being more organized in future schoolwork or to develop better study techniques. Essentially, then, procrastination is a means of self-protection and one that most students have been guilty of using at one time or another.

The downside is that through their procrastination, students miss out on many potentially enriching and growth experiences. There are many opportunities for expansion in their academic lives that students miss when they put things off.

Kathy's goal at school was to study Physiotherapy but did not get the grades to qualify. Instead, she entered the workforce, intending to enrol in Physiotherapy as a mature age student a few years later. As it turned out, she did not enrol in Physiotherapy when she qualified as a mature age student. For a number of years after that, she continually commented that she really must get around to enrolling. For a time, her procrastination served her well. People did not think she lacked the confidence or ability to study Physiotherapy. Instead, people thought she was just a terrible procrastinator. But after a while it became clear that she was probably never going to enrol and that her procrastination may be strategic and not something that 'just happened'. Eventually, people began to suspect her belief in herself and her ability to study Physiotherapy. Thus, Kathy's procrastination not only cut her off from what might have been a rewarding career (if only she believed in herself and committed whole-heartedly to her studies), but also eventually led others to suspect her ability and her motives.

It is a fact that some procrastination occurs on tasks that students know they are not going to fail. For example, some students routinely put off cleaning the bedroom. They procrastinate here not because they are frightened they will fail at it; rather, it is just that they hate doing it. However, there are other examples of procrastination in their life where it is more strategic and not just avoidance of something they do not like doing. Students must scrutinize their procrastination to determine what their motives are. One way to do this is to assess how important the task is to their self-esteem. How clean the bedroom is probably does not really affect their self-esteem, so procrastination in cleaning it is not self-protective. On the other hand, how they perform at school often does influence their self-esteem, so procrastination on schoolwork may be self-handicapping.

Interestingly, there are some students who claim to do their best study under pressure. To some extent this makes sense. Through their procrastination, they have an excuse if they fail. With their excuse at the ready, they are less anxious. With less anxiety, they perform better. This is consistent with some theories of self-handicapping suggesting that it reduces the anxiety surrounding possible failure or poor performance and leads to better performance. Unfortunately, however, the procrastinator who claims to work well under pressure is playing a dangerous game. Not all things they must do at school are amenable to procrastination. Some work simply must be completed quickly and this will place great pressure on the procrastinator. Also, in quite the opposite way, large long-term assignments or projects pose a threat to procrastinators. The longer the time frame, the more the work builds up until it is near impossible to do the work in the time remaining. Hence, procrastinators have developed a strategy that does not respond well to failure or poor performance. Invariably, failure or poor performance need to be responded to with the application of consistent and systematic effort – something the procrastinator is short on. The procrastinator's response, then, is usually limited to the strategy that got them into trouble in the first place.

In sum, procrastination is a strategy students use to deal with their fear of failure or poor performance. Procrastination may have short-term merit from a self-protection perspective. In the longer term, however, it does not help students. In adopting procrastination as their strategy, students run the very real risk of limiting their school experience. One self-handicapper summed it up: 'Procrastination just makes me miserable'. Furthermore, as a self-protection device, procrastination eventually fails students. After a time, others suspect their motives and may come to think more poorly about their abilities than should be the case.

Choosing to perform under less than ideal conditions

Another way students can self-handicap is to choose to perform under conditions that make it very difficult to succeed. Again, if they fail or perform poorly they have a ready excuse – how can anyone perform well under such difficult conditions?

In a typical study investigating this, people are given the opportunity to perform a task while listening to music they believe will improve their performance or while listening to music they believe will interfere with their performance. It has been found that people who fear failure or poor performance are more likely to elect to perform the task while listening to music they believe will interfere with their performance. That is, people actually choose to perform under conditions that they know will interfere with their performance. This is so that they can deflect the cause of this failure or poor performance away from their incompetence and onto the music.

The educational context provides countless examples. Why do some students take calculators into their final maths exam with fading batteries, despite their teachers repeatedly warning them before the exam to use new batteries? Why do some students study with distracting music on? Why do some students forget to bring their textbooks home to study the night before an important exam? From a self-protection perspective, these are all a means of establishing excuses that can be used if they perform poorly.

The use of alcohol and other drugs to self-handicap

The early research into self-handicapping looked at how people drink alcohol before engaging in a task they fear they will perform poorly. By drinking, they can blame the poor performance on the alcohol rather than their incompetence. By protecting their competence, they have protected their worth and self-esteem. Since that early research on alcohol, researchers have looked at how people use other drugs before a performance situation. In this type of research, study participants are given the choice to take a performance-improving drug or a performance-harming drug (in fact, they are not given real drugs – they are simply led to believe that they are real drugs) prior to having to perform on a particular task. Sure enough, people who fear failure or poor performance tend to choose the performance-harming drug. Why? Because they are able to blame their failure or poor performance on the drug rather than their incompetence. Now that their competence is not in question, neither is their self-esteem. They protect their self-esteem.

As with all types of self-handicapping, Self-handicapping through alcohol or other drugs may work for a while. However, not only is it harmful for the developing brain and body, as it becomes a consistent feature of behaviour others begin to suspect that the alcohol is hiding some weakness. In effect, the strategy turns from being a perceived alibi to being a curse. It might have protected for a while, but there comes a time when it quite clearly does not. The longer the self-handicapping goes on, the harder the cycle is to break.

Letting themselves get rundown

Another way students self-handicap is by letting themselves get rundown and then using their poor condition as an excuse if they perform poorly. It may be that they burn the candle at both ends and get tired and fatigued. It may be that they maintain a poor diet and get out of shape. Under focus here is where students let themselves become rundown and become tired or worn-out.

Highly familiar are the students who push themselves in their studies to such an extent that by the time the exam comes around, they are too exhausted to perform well. These students cannot be accused of not studying hard. Quite the contrary; these students went above and beyond the call of duty. This is a reversal of students who do not study at all. But interestingly, both are forms of self-handicapping. One student uses his lack of study as an excuse to protect his worth. The other can use her fatigue through too much study as an excuse to protect her worth. We see, then, that extremes of the one activity can be used strategically to protect self-esteem in response to a fear of failure or poor performance.

Essentially, then, what both students lack is balance. In fact, they try to avoid balance at all costs. This is because balance provides the fairest test of competence. If students invest a realistic and sensible amount of study then if they fail or performs poorly they cannot use a lack of study as the reason, nor can they blame exhaustion due to excessive study. Basically, when students perform under conditions of balance, then those conditions lend themselves to the fairest test of their competence and the ideal chance for success. It is clear, then, why students fearing failure or poor performance go to extreme lengths to avoid balance and a fair test.

In fact, this issue of balance is revisited a few times in this book. It is shown later that students can set standards too low or too high in a bid to protect their self-esteem. Similarly, it will be shown later that students tackle tasks that are either too easy or too difficult or set expectations that are too low or too high. In all cases, balance is missing because it is balance that provides the best and fairest test of competence. Sometimes, best and fairest tests of competence are the last things students want.

How can we tell if students may be strategically letting themselves get rundown? Ask the following questions. When students have an important upcoming event in which they are required to perform in some way, do they:

- get enough sleep?
- eat well?
- empty their plate of unnecessary stresses?
- get a sensible amount of rest?

Or, do they:

- stay up late?
- eat poorly?
- give equal (or more) priority to unnecessary stresses?
- work too hard with little or no time for rest and relaxation?

If the answer is 'no' to any of the first set of questions and 'yes' to any of the second set, then students need to ask themselves why this is the case. Why are they not giving their body and mind a fair chance at success?

One line of questioning would be to ask, what are the consequences of failing or performing poorly in the context of little sleep, rest, relaxation or a poor diet? It may be that these provide excuses that shift the cause of failure or poor performance away from possible incompetence and onto fatigue or their rundown state. Again, because their competence is not in question, neither is their self-esteem. It may be because they are perfectionistic or overstrivers – again, approaches under-pinned by a fear of failure.

'Claytons' self-handicapping

Now I lie about it. I lied the other day when I was asked why I crammed for the exam. I said that I had to work the last three days and I didn't.

Francis, age 18

Thus far, active self-handicapping has been the focus of discussion. This type of self-handicapping involves setting up real obstacles to chances of success. Being unprepared is a real obstacle. Little or no study is a real obstacle.

Sometimes, however, students only look like they are self-handicapping when in reality they are not. Here, this is called Claytons self-handicapping: the self-handicapping students do when they are not self-handicapping, named after a non-alcoholic drink popular in the 1970s ('the drink you have when you're not having a drink').

It was once said that people make of their adversity what suits their purposes. Claytons self-handicappers are masters at this. They use past experiences and current circumstances to avoid present responsibility. What are some examples?

In the educational context, students might tell people that they are more anxious about a test than they really are. Exaggerating their anxiety is a way of telling others that there is an obstacle (anxiety) present but not actually suffering the level of anxiety they are reporting. So, they have an excuse ready without actually hindering their performance. Similarly, students might turn up to an important exam and say that they have not studied when in fact they have.

In each case, students are strategically manoeuvring to protect their self-esteem in case they do not do as well as they would like. In some respects, this self-handicapping could be seen as ideal because students are not actually putting an obstacle in place and yet they have the luxury of an excuse if they fail. It seems as though they can have the best of both worlds.

Unfortunately for many students, it is not as simple as this. What has been found is that the students who tend to use Claytons self-handicapping are at risk of using real self-handicapping. That is, students can have difficulty using one and not the other. For this reason, Claytons self-handicapping is treated in much the same way as real self-handicapping is treated. Thus, the strategies later presented to overcome self-handicapping are the same for both its real and Claytons forms.

Claytons self-handicapping focuses students' minds on their limitations and the possibility of failure or poor performance rather than on their strengths and the possibility of success. Countless studies have shown that when students focus on their limitations, focus on failure or poor performance, and hold negative expectations, they perform more poorly, are less motivated, and are less likely to enjoy what they do. So, even if Claytons self-handicapping is not real self-handicapping and even though students do not actively put obstacles in their path, it is not as harmless as they might first think.

To what extent are students Claytons self-handicappers? Ask the following questions. When students have to perform on an important task or activity, do they tell people that:

- they have not prepared when they really have?
- they are more anxious than they really are?
- they are more tired than they really are?
- they are more run down than they really are?
- past events are affecting what they do more than is really the case?
- they have not prepared when they really have?

If the answer to some, most or all these questions is 'yes', then students may be sabotaging some areas of their lives when they really need not.

Conclusion

Self-handicapping is a way of setting up excuses in case of poor performance or failure. Students usually do this in response to their fear of failure or poor performance. Because their cleverness and competence are how they define their self-esteem, failure (that reflects incompetence) is a real threat to that self-esteem. By self-handicapping, students can blame their failure on the obstacle and not on their possible incompetence. In doing so, they protect their self-esteem. For example, students can blame their poor exam performance on their procrastination or their lack of study.

Some students engage in 'Claytons' self-handicapping. This is where they claim an obstacle exists when it does not or where they exaggerate the difficulties in their academic life. This obstacle or adversity is then used as the excuse if they perform poorly or fail. Students may report that they are more anxious than they really are before an exam. If they do not perform well, they can blame the anxiety. Students may tell others that they are more rundown or tired than they really are before they do a test. In the event that they perform poorly or fail, they can blame the reported handicap. At first glance, Claytons self-handicapping may look like a no lose situation – students have an excuse available without really self-handicapping. But real and Claytons self-handicapping are closely connected and Claytons self-handicapping often occurs alongside some real self-handicapping. Also, Claytons self-handicapping puts students' focus on their shortcomings, fears and doubts and these are by no means ideal conditions under which to perform.

For a time self-handicapping may serve its desired purpose; that is, others – and indeed some students themselves – believe the handicap is the reason why they performed poorly. But after a while, self-handicapping is viewed with suspicion. Others suspect that it is a cover-up for insecurities, incompetence or both. More importantly, students get caught in a vicious cycle of failure or poor performance, where they increasingly cut themselves off from any hope of success.

In the longer term, it would have been much better for students if they had tackled their fear of failure or poor performance in a more positive, success-focused way. It is critical to understand that self-handicapping is a pattern of behaviour that can be broken. Part 4 looks at the ways students can address self-handicapping and embrace school life with a motivation to achieve success rather than a motivation to avoid failure or poor performance. This is a critical distinction. It is critical because a focus on success carries with it greater happiness, satisfaction with school life, motivation and confidence.

6

DEFENSIVE PESSIMISM AND DEFENSIVE OPTIMISM

> I try to be pessimistic because that way I think the fall's less when you do actually 'come-a-cropper'... You just try to minimize those falls
>
> Robert, age 17

In Chapter 5 we looked at self-defeating behaviours that can be used as an excuse in case students fail. By having an excuse, their self-esteem lives to see another day. On the downside, however, self-defeating behaviour also leads to negative academic outcomes. If students handicap their chances of academic success, they are less likely to succeed. Indeed, research shows that this is in fact the case.

This chapter moves on from self-defeating behaviour to examine self-defeating thinking. In response to potential failure and fear of it, students can engage in problematic thinking that might rescue them if failure occurs, but can have negative academic consequences as well. Two patterns of thinking are examined in this chapter: defensive pessimism and defensive optimism.

Defensive pessimism

Defensive pessimists set unrealistically low expectations for themselves, usually leading up to a performance or evaluation of some sort; that is, they lower the bar on themselves even though they are capable of performing at a higher level. Or, they may lower the bar on themselves even though they have done okay in the past.

Some examples of defensive pessimism include:

- telling yourself or others that you are going to fail the test or exam, when you have done okay in the past
- aiming for a C grade, when you are capable of an A or a B grade
- shooting for a pass grade, when you are capable of higher
- telling yourself and others you will be happy just to get through the course, when you have the capacity to do more than this
- being negative about your future academic prospects, when there is reason to be positive
- taking on a pass study unit when you are capable of taking an advanced study unit

- believing you are not capable of school-related responsibilities (e.g. student representative or prefect), when you are capable of performing in these roles
- telling yourself that you will not make friends in your new class, when you have made friends with others before

Looking closely at these examples, it is evident that this pessimism is a particular type of pessimism. It is unrealistic. It is pessimism when there is little or no realistic basis for it. It is pessimism that flies in the face of the evidence; that is, students are lowering their expectations despite the fact that they are capable of striving for and attaining higher expectations. Why do they do this?

We find these students are fearful of failing and are motivated to avoid failure. Despite previous adequate performance, they doubt their capacity to perform next time. No matter how well they have performed in the past, they are fearful they cannot perform well today or tomorrow. Irrespective of their ability, they fear they do not have what it takes to achieve to their ability. Regardless of their capacity to take advanced course options, they fear they are not up to the task.

Reasons for defensive pessimism

Why do students set low expectations and goals when it is clear that they have good reason to expect better of themselves? Research shows that they do so for a few reasons and each one is a way of dealing with fear of failure and its consequences.

The first reason students engage in defensive pessimism is so they lower the bar and thereby make failure less likely. If students only aim for a C grade at school, they are less likely to fail against this goal than if they aim for a B or A grade. If students say they are not going to be perfect, then it is less likely to be considered a failure if they do not become perfect. If students say they are only going to get fourth or fifth in the class, then they are less likely to 'fail' than if they held the expectation that they are going to come first. If students say they will not improve in a school subject, then they are less likely to 'fail' than if they held the positive expectation that they will improve. If students do not expect to make any friends in their new class, then they are less likely to 'fail' than if they expect they will make friends. Basically, if students lower the bar, then it is easier for them to jump over it. So, defensive pessimists deal with their fear of failure by making failure less likely.

The second reason students are defensive pessimists is so they reduce the disappointment they might experience if they do fail. According to the defensive pessimist, if they aim high they are more likely to be disappointed than if they aim low. If students expect a C grade, they are less likely to be disappointed when they get a C grade. On the other hand, if they expect an A grade, they are likely to be disappointed if they get a B or a C grade. If a student does not expect to make any friends in their new class, they are less likely to be disappointed if they actually do not make any friends. On the other hand, if they expect to be Ms Popularity, then few or no friends is likely to be quite a disappointment.

Hence, defensive pessimists aim to reduce the chances of disappointment wherever possible. They try to protect their emotions from failure. As Robert went on to say, 'If I do worse than expected, then it's less of a fall'. Or, according to Dianne, age 17, her defensive pessimism reduced the potential blow to her self-esteem by not 'thinking that you're going to reach the moon when you can only get as far as the clouds'.

Another reason students are defensive pessimists is so they prepare themselves and others for failure. Failure is not so hard-hitting when it is expected and one is braced for it. Defensive pessimists are the students reminding their parents that they said they were not going to do well in that test. 'Didn't I warn you?' they will protest if they get a poor result. In fact, students can be quite expert at preparing their parents for possible failure. 'Don't get angry with me! I told you I was going to screw up that exam!' they will retort if a bad grade comes in.

Defensive pessimism is also a way to keep pressure from others at bay. Some students find there is such extreme pressure placed on them to perform well that they need to engage in protective behaviour to help them through.

According to Gwen, by lowering expectations she believes it is a way to reduce others' expectations of her so she can feel more comfortable in her academic life. It is also a way to minimize the pain if she performs below expectations – even if she has disappointed her parents, at least she is not so disappointed.

For some students, defensive pessimism may also be an appeal for help. In some cases, students who share their negative expectations with friends and family may receive positive messages from these significant others, leaving them feeling better about things. For example, family members might challenge the pessimism by communicating their confidence in the student and identifying the student's past successes in similar situations. Or, they may simply recognize the student's fears, leaving them feeling better understood and not so alone as they face their challenges. In more substantial cases, the student may be communicating negative expectations as a more serious flag for anxiety, depression or significant skill deficiencies (e.g. a reading difficulty). In such cases, more substantial assistance and intervention is needed.

It is also important to recognize that students can develop their defensive pessimism as a result of powerful messages from significant others. Marie, age 17, for example, reported that her negativity was learnt at home: 'My parents have always said, 'Don't set your goals too high because you'll only get disappointed' ... They're always careful not to raise my hopes so I don't get disappointed'. Other students may be caught between significant others (e.g. teachers) who seek to boost their confidence and encourage positive expectations and significant others (e.g. home) who are reluctant to foster positivity in the student. According to Theresa, age 17, 'Some people are telling me, "You're doing well", then I go home and my Dad says, "I'm not going to praise you because it's going to go to your head". So I'm kind of in two worlds. I don't know who to believe'.

The reasons provided thus far are all protective in nature. They serve to protect the student from the fear or impact of failure. Because of this, it can be a seductive strategy for those who believe they are not up to the task of striving for and attaining more positive expectations. There is, however, another seductive aspect of defensive pessimism. This relates to the potentially enhancing properties of defensive pessimism.

If setting unrealistically low expectations can protect students when they do not perform so well, then the opposite must also be the case – they will be pleasantly surprised if they do better than they expect. Shooting for a C grade and receiving a B grade will evoke positive feelings and reactions. Aiming for a pass, but doing much better will feel good. Getting over the line when you have convinced others you are going to fail will elicit positive responses. These are what we call the enhancing properties of defensive pessimism. Again, as Robert tells us, 'I think if I border slightly on the pessimistic, then if I do better than I expected, it's a pleasant surprise'. According to Samantha, age 17, 'I've never been one to set my goals too high. I keep them sub-low. So I will be surprised'.

In a nutshell, defensive pessimism deals with a fear of failure by reducing the likelihood of failure, reducing the disappointment if failure occurs, and preparing the students and others for failure so that they are less accountable for that failure. In the event that the student performs above expectation, there is cause for positive emotion and a positive response both personally and with significant others.

> Richard, age 14, a middle school student, is a defensive pessimist in mathematics. Despite being good with numbers, he is pessimistic about the mark he will get in the math test this semester. This has a number of advantages. For a start, he has set a lower standard that is easier to reach (he has lowered the bar) – so 'failure' is less likely. Second, by being pessimistic, he cushions himself from the blow of a poor result if it should occur – in a sense, he has prepared himself for a poor result so that it is not so hard-hitting. His defensive pessimism is a way he can reduce the likelihood of performing poorly, or at least prepare himself for the disappointment if he does. If Richard performs higher than he has been telling himself and his parents, he is likely to get a favourable reaction from them and be pleasantly surprised himself.

Consequences of defensive pessimism

On first blush, it seems students have nothing to lose by this strategy – protection in the case of poor performance and enhancement in the case of positive performance. As with self-handicapping, however, all is not as it seems. As seductive as defensive pessimism may appear, there is a price to pay.

As with most self-protective strategies, there is a dark side to defensive pessimism. As students set lower and lower expectations, goals, or standards, they run the risk of performing in that direction. The fact is, students often only do as much as they expect of themselves. So, if students do not expect to perform well in an upcoming test, they are likely to be less enthusiastic, less energetic, less likely to try hard, and less 'switched on' in the test. This is supported by defensive pessimists' own reports. For example, Ava, age 17, reported that she would 'jump straight in and write the first thing that comes to mind' and Emily, age 16, commented that 'if something bores me, I just write the first thing that comes to mind'.

On the other hand, if students go in with confidence, they are more inclined to behave in ways consistent with this through more enthusiasm, more energy, and more effort. According to Lynne, age 16, an optimistic student, 'I organize a little timetable for myself. I have every half hour accounted for and I'd set my alarm so I wouldn't go over time'. Bernadette, age 18, another optimist, reported, 'basically when I'm on a roll, I feel good. I think, "Well I've got this mark and I can do it again."'

Another dark side to defensive pessimism is that it is often accompanied by some unpleasant emotions and thoughts. Defensive pessimists tend to be very anxious, high in self-doubt, low in self-esteem and low in hope. These are not very pleasant emotions and thoughts to travel through school with. Additionally, these emotions and thoughts further reduce students' ability to perform successfully. Helena's (age 17) experience of study is that 'if I think negative, then everything will turn out negative for me. Whereas ... I've [since] thought about things positively, I haven't got stressed about things, and things have worked out for the best'.

Yet another dark side is the long-term impact of habitual defensive pessimism. Some students can get into such a downward spiral of negative expectations that they actually experience a run of poor performance or failure. These students have not been successful in the last five tests. It is at this point that they might abandon their defensive pessimism for a more dramatic way to deal with failure. One such strategy is self-handicapping. As described earlier, they might start behaving (not just thinking) in ways that jeopardize their academic success. They might start routinely missing class or turning up late to exams. Thus, if not tackled quickly and effectively, defensive pessimism can become a slippery slope to more problematic behaviour.

Defensive pessimism can also have negative social effects.

Some students have reported that after a while their friends and family get tired of hearing about their negative expectations. Friends start thinking the student is a 'downer' to be around. Furthermore, if the student actually performs well in the face of negative expectations, friends become irritated, suspect the student is not being genuine, begin questioning the student's motives for reporting negative expectations, and are less responsive to the student. In the case of family, if the student performs well or is capable of performing well, parents may switch off from the negative self-talk. This can be risky because there are times when children are in genuine need or difficulty and require parental responsiveness. In a sense, 'crying wolf' may ultimately leave the student exposed.

'Claytons' defensive pessimism

Thus far, active defensive pessimism has been the focus. It has addressed situations where students genuinely fear failure, genuinely fear they do not have what it takes to do well, and genuinely lower their expectations in the face of counter-evidence. Sometimes, however, students report negative expectations but do not actually believe the negative expectations they are communicating. As with disingenuous self-handicapping, this is called 'Claytons' defensive pessimism: defensive pessimism students report when they are not really defensive pessimists.

Claytons defensive pessimists will report negative expectations when they actually believe they will do just fine. Or, they may exaggerate their negativity about a particular performance or evaluation situation. The important point here is that some students are authentic in their negative expectations while others stretch the negativity strategically. Thus, defensive pessimists have low expectations when they are capable of more. Claytons defensive pessimists set low expectations when they are capable of achieving more and believe they can achieve more. What are some examples?

A student might tell his parents that he will fail the assignment, when he actually believes this will not be the case. Similarly, a student might turn up to an important exam telling friends she will barely pass, when she privately knows she will do much better than this. In some respects, Claytons defensive pessimism could be seen as ideal because students are not actually caught up in genuine negativity but at the same time can reap self-enhancing benefits if they do succeed. It seems as though they can have the best of both worlds.

However, as with the Claytons self-handicapper, it is not as simple as this. It has been found that students who use Claytons defensive pessimism are at risk of moving into more genuine negativity. It can become difficult to use one and not the other. Claytons defensive pessimism runs the risk of focusing students' minds on the possibility of failure or poor performance rather than on their strengths and the possibility of success. Countless studies have shown that when students focus on their limitations, focus on failure and hold negative expectations, they perform more poorly, are less motivated, and enjoy what they do less. So, even if Claytons defensive pessimism is not real defensive pessimism and even though Claytons defensive pessimists do not believe their self-reported negative expectations, it is not as harmless as they might think.

Defensive optimism

Interestingly, at the other end of the defensive pessimism continuum is defensive optimism. Defensive optimists set unrealistically high expectations for themselves; that is, despite counter-evidence and past track record, they believe they will perform highly in the next task or challenge. This is not to be confused with realistic optimism where students set the bar a touch ahead of where they are at present. Realistic optimism is helpful optimism because it is optimism grounded in reality based on positive expectations that are realistically attainable. In contrast, the defensive optimist sets expectations way too high and counter to what should be expected of them.

Examples of defensive optimism include:

- striving for a Top 5 rank in the class when all prior performance has placed them towards the bottom
- selecting books or texts that are obviously too far ahead of any previous attainment
- shooting for an A grade when no prior result has been above a C grade
- nominating university or college courses that are not suited to a student's school subject selection or interests

- working on computer tasks or activities very much above one's difficulty level

The problem with defensive optimism is not so much the optimism; rather, it is the extreme or unrealistic nature of the optimism and the fact that it is defensively motivated that is problematic. Thus, students should not be urged to abandon optimism. Instead, they should be encouraged towards optimism that is a closer reflection of where they are now and where they can be in the short to medium term.

Hence, based on the above defensive optimism examples, realistic optimism would involve:

- striving for a mid-range rank in the class when prior performance has placed them towards the bottom
- selecting books or texts that are a touch ahead of any previous attainment so that the level of challenge is maintained but the level of difficulty is not overwhelming
- shooting for a B grade when prior results have been a C grade or below
- nominating university or college courses that are suited to a student's school subject selection and interests
- working on computer tasks or activities at one's challenge level but not above one's difficulty level

When these proximal or close-range goals are met, the student can then raise the bar again. Indeed, it is very possible for students to ultimately attain what was originally a defensively optimistic goal.

Reasons for defensive optimism

It is proposed that defensive optimism is yet another response to fear of failure and academic insecurity. First, rather than having to deal with the possibility of failure, some students find it preferable to live in a form of denial. Optimism in the face of counter-evidence is one way to avoid having to contemplate or consider failure. It is also a way to avoid having to consider one's limitations and weaknesses. If students insist on holding positive expectations that are not based on the reality of likely poorer performance, then for a time they avoid the discomfort of possible poor performance and their own limitations in relation to this.

Following from this, defensive optimism is also a way to protect one's self-esteem and self-worth – at least for a while. As we now know, in the academic context one of the greatest threats to self-worth is academic failure and judgements of incompetence. To the extent that students can distract the focus from poor performance and personal limitations, for a time they can protect their self-worth.

As discussed in the self-handicapping chapter, defensive optimism can also be a way of establishing an excuse for poor performance. Students can 'blame' the high expectation rather than their inability to meet the high expectation: very few people could attain such a high standard, so the student cannot be held to account for not attaining it either. In this case, the student's main mistake is setting an unrealistically high expectation or standard, not failing to attain them. In so doing, they cannot be accused of lacking the ability to attain the goal, simply of getting the target wrong. Now that their ability is off the hook, so is their self-worth. Thus, setting unrealistically high expectations in this case has been a way of self-worth protection.

Grace, age 17, is in her last year of school, approaching her final exams. In conjunction with the marks she obtained in her mid-year exams, these finals determine her post-school pathway in terms of what university and what course she will get into. Throughout her high school years, she has doggedly stuck to the idea of studying Architecture at university – a course in high demand and thus requiring a high entrance mark. Based on the early and middle years of high school – and then confirmed in the senior years – Grace was a mid-range performer, but not up to the level required for a high-ranking university course. While she held onto her plans with little regard for the fact she might be on the wrong track, she did not have to face up to a possible lack of ability and was not faced with the damage this might cause her self-esteem and self-worth. In this sense, her defensive optimism served its purpose. However, alongside this, she moved into senior high school with little regard for the possibility she might not make it into Architecture, little consideration of how she might need to improve herself to gain entry to this high-ranking university course, and little thought as to whether another course

> would be more appropriate. Thus, although she may have protected her self-worth for a while, she also progressively cut herself off from other possible attractive and realistic opportunities.

It should be emphasized that Grace's problem was not optimism. Rather, it was the level of optimism that exceeded all evidence by too great a degree. It was also the motivation for her optimism – a defensive, self-protective optimism that suggested trouble. A consistent and measured optimism motivated by a positive desire to extend herself would have served her better, kept her options open, and allowed her to attain a post-school pathway in keeping with her personal potential.

Consequences of defensive optimism

It should first be acknowledged that some extreme optimists pull it off. The consequence of their high levels of optimism is success. They actually attain the high expectations that at first appeared totally unrealistic. In actual fact, it may be that these students are not really defensive optimists. Because these students are often energized, enthusiastic, forward-looking and reasonably confident it seems they are not defensive at all. They are proactive rather than defensive, on the front foot rather than the back foot, and keen to get ahead rather than protect themselves. Students who reflect this profile are not relevant to this discussion of defensive optimism – they reflect success seeking, discussed earlier.

It should also be acknowledged that defensive optimism has protective value. It can protect self-worth, it can give a student the sense that the situation is not dire or problematic in any major way (a false security), and it can defer any unpleasant introspection or soul-searching that might need to happen. From these perspectives, it serves its purpose.

But there are costs to defensive optimism. First, stubbornly and defensively adhering to unrealistically high expectations when all indicators suggest a need to look closely at one's situation means valuable opportunities to learn from mistakes may be lost. A very important part of academic success requires students to look frankly and fearlessly at setback, disappointment, dashed hopes and unrealized expectations. A student who has had a run of poor grades in science would do well to look at what is needed to address this. Little or no regard for the reality and rigidly sticking to expectations that might need revision greatly increases the chances this student will stay stuck in this run of poor results. As any success story in any field of human endeavour will show, a capacity to learn from mistakes is paramount.

The defensive optimist may also be missing out on valuable help from others. Defensively based optimism at unrealistic levels does not leave much room for constructive criticism, helpful suggestions, or other types of guidance. In fact, defensive optimism is almost antithetical to assistance. To be receptive to assistance would pose too great a threat to the student whose optimism is motivated by a need to deny or ignore any limitations or weakness. Thus, it is not unusual to find it very difficult to give any sort of advice to these students. Their defensive walls are up and the thought of weakness is threatening on many levels. Returning to Grace, there were many attempts in junior and middle high school to identify and work on some of the factors underpinning some of her poor performance. However, while the self-protective dynamics and motivation were present, Grace was not receptive to these efforts.

Another consequence of defensive optimism is poor person-environment fit. Person-environment fit refers to how well suited individuals are to their environment. The workplace is one of the main areas under focus in person-environment fit research. This research looks at how well suited employees are to particular jobs and occupations. When there is a good fit, employees are happy, mentally healthy, and satisfied in their work. When there is poor fit, we find the opposite. One of the factors that determines good fit relates to the goals people set. Those whose goals are well matched to who they are, their capabilities and their prior experience tend to find better fit in the things they do. The goals students have for work are very much shaped at school – through the subjects they take, the level of subject difficulty, the grades they receive, and the messages they receive from teachers. This is where things can go awry for defensive optimists. They do not make good plans, are not receptive to information needed to set appropriate goals, and as a result can land in post-school courses or jobs that do not suit them – that is, defensive optimism can lead to poor choices and poor person-environment fit.

As with defensive pessimists, there can also be a social price to pay for defensive optimism. Students whose optimism is high but defensively motivated can be difficult to interact with. It is difficult dealing with a student who always seems to know best and whose defensiveness means they cannot be shown otherwise. It is difficult to stay committed to a student who is never receptive to constructive criticism or constructive feedback. The risk here is that defensively optimistic students become more isolated from the people and support known to enhance and sustain academic health.

Conclusion

Defensive pessimism refers to the unrealistically low expectations set by some students. Students usually do this in response to their fear of failure or need to avoid poor performance. Through defensive pessimism, students can set lower expectations that are easier to attain, reduce disappointment if they do fail, and prepare themselves and others for failure if it should occur. These are all a means of protecting them in case they fail or make failure less likely because they have set safe and easy standards to shoot for.

Other students engage in defensive optimism. This is where students set unrealistically high expectations that are defensively motivated. In doing this, students can pin possible failure on the high standard they set (not their lack of ability), avoid uncomfortable self-evaluation, and not have to deal with any possible threat to their self-worth.

There can be protective benefits from defensive pessimism and defensive optimism. For a while, students may render failure less likely, they can avoid potentially painful introspection, they may cushion the blow of poor performance, and protect their self-worth. But after a while, there is a price to pay through potentially declining achievement, lost opportunities to learn, little courageous self-examination that can improve them, and even social costs among friends and family.

In the longer term, it would have been better for these

students if they had tackled their fear of failure or poor performance in a more proactive and courageous way. Defensive pessimism and defensive optimism are patterns of thought that can be broken, but only when their causal factors are tackled. Part 4 of this book examines these factors and the ways teachers and students can address them.

7

DISENGAGEMENT AND HELPLESSNESS

There are stages when I think, 'I'm going to drop out. I can't do this anymore.

> Jodie, age 18

I couldn't be bothered and I don't know if I am going to stay. I'm sort of sick of it.

> Patrick, age 17

I knew from Day 1 I was depressed and I didn't want to be here. It was a waste of time.

> Ellie, age 18

Academic helplessness and disengagement occurs when students believe there is nothing they can do to avoid failing and there is nothing they can do to attain or repeat success; that is, they believe academic outcomes are beyond their control. They believe they have no say in how well they do. They do not feel in the driver's seat and as a result feel and behave in ways that reflect helplessness and disengagement.

Disengagement often results from a run of poor performances or unpleasant academic experiences and is coupled with a very pessimistic and hopeless outlook. Because of this, it is important to not only try to change the student's experiences in some way so that the cycle of unpleasantness is cut (at least for a while) but to also try to shift their extreme negativity and hopelessness.

To be frank, these students are the hardest to shift. These are the students who have little or no interest in school or schoolwork, do not care if they fail, do not care if they drop out of school (or get kicked out), or firmly believe that anything they try to do turns out badly. They fully believe they are going to fail and have become helpless in the face of this.

In many cases, these students may not even be bothered to cause any trouble in the classroom or school. They may hope for a private understanding with the teacher that if they do not cause the teacher any trouble, the teacher will not cause them any trouble, and then eventually the whole school thing will be over.

Helplessness and disengagement often peaks in the middle high school years. Teachers will often report that these are the toughest years to teach. In primary school, students tend to be bright-eyed and bushy tailed (but not all of them), in junior high school students are reasonably interested (but not all of them); and in senior high school they mature a bit and have chosen to stay on (but not all of them). The middle high years (when students are about 14–15 years of age) are more challenging for teachers and parents. Having said this, there are children gazing out the classroom window at age 6 and there are senior high school students doing little or no schoolwork.

Sliding down the fear and failure slope

Another reason for disengagement is that all other attempts to avoid fear and failure have been unsuccessful. Students can slide through a cycle of fear of failure and into helplessness or disengagement. This slide might begin with overstriving or perfectionism (discussed in the next chapter) where students try to avoid failure by succeeding. There are, however, some students for whom this does not work and the threat of failure looms a little larger. At this point they may opt for a more defensive way to deal with their fear – defensive pessimism being one such strategy. The risk of defensive pessimism is that students can come to do only as much as they expect of themselves and if this is the case, as they lower the bar on themselves, their achievement may lower as well. At this point they may conclude that if they cannot avoid failure then at least they can avoid the implications of failure and have an excuse for it, and so begin self-handicapping. Unfortunately, self-handicapping can lose its appeal because after a while the excuses run out. With nowhere left to run, the last option is to disengage from the very thing that is causing all this heartache – school.

Forms of disengagement and helplessness

Helplessness and disengagement can take many forms, including:

- absenteeism and school refusal
- dropping out of school
- refusing to do schoolwork
- giving up on a continual basis
- never completing schoolwork
- lacking any interest in school-related activities and tasks
- lacking any care and attention in schoolwork

In each case, the students are not at all engaged in their school life. Some forms of disengagement are quite dramatic and distressing. It is very distressing for parents to have children who refuse to go to school because they feel helpless to succeed or are disengaged from the work. Even more distressing is the situation where a student ends up dropping out of school due to disengagement and helplessness.

Leading to these 'end-of-the-line' forms of disengagement are more daily forms of disengagement that make life very difficult for student and teacher alike. Students who refuse to do schoolwork during class can be extremely frustrating students to teach. Students who constantly give up in their schoolwork or do their work quickly without any care or attention can wear a teacher down over the course of weeks and months. Students who lack any interest or enthusiasm for subject matter are difficult to teach.

It is also useful to think about academic disengagement at four levels:

1. *Cognitive (or attitudinal) disengagement*: this refers to students' thoughts of disengagement such as 'There's no point in trying', 'There's no way I can succeed', 'I might as well give up'.

2. *Behavioural disengagement*: this is where students behave in disengaged ways. Cutting class, doing no schoolwork, refusing to do homework and assignments, and not listening in lessons are some examples of behavioural disengagement.

3. *Emotional disengagement*: this refers to students emotionally detaching from school and schoolwork. Examples of emotional disengagement include hating school, being angry with teacher requests and expectations, fearing school and school attendance, and perhaps emotionally attaching to anti-school peers.

4. *Schematic disengagement*: schemas are more deeply held personal views and values, and in some ways represent a more profound disengagement. Examples of schema disengagement are 'School is not for me', 'All teachers are out to fail me', 'School won't get me anywhere', and 'Learning is pointless'.

To some extent, schema disengagement is the most troubling of all. It could be considered the cumulative effect of the other three forms of disengagement. Research suggests that students can shift their cognition (attitude), behaviour and emotion, but it is more difficult to shift schemas. It is therefore vital that cognitive, behavioural and emotional disengagement are not allowed to take root for too long because negative shifts in schemas can have big impacts. For example, it is relatively easier to change a student's thinking about a specific school subject than it is to change their view that school is pointless.

Problem cycles leading to disengagement and helplessness

Ongoing disengagement runs the very real risk of building into a fast-moving negative feedback loop, as follows:

1. Carl, age 14, displays a lack of interest in maths.
2. His teacher, Mrs Klein, responds negatively to this by expressing her frustration with Carl in front of the class.
3. This confirms in Carl's mind that this subject and Mrs Klein are not for him and he now displays an antagonism towards her and all class activities.
4. Mrs Klein now becomes somewhat hostile to Carl, angry that this one student is ruining what might otherwise be a good class.
5. Carl starts cutting class.
6. Mrs Klein and the school are required to demand that Carl attends class.
7. Carl gives it one more go, but because everyone's nerves are frayed, this unravels with rapid force.
8. Carl is put on suspension, further alienating him from this class and school generally.
9. There is an attempt to engage Carl with an action plan on his return, but because there is now too much negative history, this is unsuccessful and Carl is asked to leave.

In this sequence, we have what might be called a 'coercive cycle of relations'. Each party bounces off the other in a negative and coercive way. With each iteration, the coercion becomes more extreme until breaking point. In many cases, students will drop out or be asked to leave. In some cases, teachers can take it no longer and ask to be moved to another class or move to another school. In more drastic cases, teachers will drop out of teaching. There is a long line of research demonstrating teacher attrition that is often a result of student disengagement that takes coercive or hostile forms.

There are other possible negative feedback loops. One relates to quiet underachievement, as follows:

---

1. Kerry, age 14, has been receiving borderline grades, is losing confidence and becoming unsure she can improve things.
2. Her teacher, Mr. Dorban, gives what help he can, but with a demanding class and additional duties at school, assistance is limited.
3. Kerry's grades drop some more, her self-doubt becomes more entrenched, and she starts feeling helpless.
4. Kerry's helplessness means she does not seek further help, does not make any noises to indicate she is struggling, and becomes something of a quiet underachiever.
5. Because the class has a couple of behaviour problems that take most of Mr Dorban's extra time, quiet underachievers like Kerry fly under his radar.
6. It is only at the end-of-year report time that Kerry's parents realize she has been bumping along the bottom for the better part of two terms, by which time Kerry is emotionally, attitudinally and behaviourally disengaged from school.

Clearly, Kerry's is a different sequence to Carl's. Kerry represents quite a substantial group of students who quietly disengage and quietly slip away at school never performing to potential, never picked up, never quite understood – and too often paying a price through life because of this. The squeaky hinge usually gets oil – and so the likes of Kerry do not get the oil they need. However, what is similar across both Kerry and Carl is a growing sense of helplessness, a progressive disaffection from school, and a conclusion to school life that is utterly unsatisfying and unsatisfactory.

These examples give clues as to why students disengage from school and schoolwork. Some students have quite negative experiences with teachers and if this is not resolved, they distance themselves from school and schoolwork. Some students have learning difficulties or distinct learning needs that are not picked up and they underachieve to a point of withdrawal. Some experience such chronic poor performance that they see no way out or no bright light on their academic horizon. Some who are low in confidence do not receive the sort of ongoing encouragement needed to get on in school. To varying degrees, each of these is reflected in the stories of Carl and Kerry above. There are, however, other reasons for disengagement that are not so evident in those sequences. These relate to a lack of control, developmental stages during high school, modelling by parents and teachers, poor fit between the student and school, poor mental health and social problems. Each of these discussed now.

Low control

A low sense of control is one of the most consistently identified predictors of helplessness and disengagement. When students believe they cannot influence outcomes in their academic life they start to feel helplessness. When this is backed up by a run of poor performance, the rot can set in and students may give up.

A number of things lead to a student's loss of control. One particularly powerful factor is the way students see the causes of their academic outcomes; that is, the way students explain why something happened can affect their sense of control. This is referred to as students' explanatory style. Explanatory style is the students' typical way of explaining events and outcomes in their academic life. One aspect of students' explanatory style relates to the extent to which they see their academic life as controllable. Examples of controllable factors include how much work they do, how they do that work, where they do that work, the presentation of their work and so on. Examples of uncontrollable factors include the difficulty of test questions, good or bad luck, the teacher's marking and so on. The more students focus on the controllable factors in their life, the more control they will feel. The more they focus on factors that are uncontrollable, the more they are at risk of helplessness. If you follow the logic: if students believe they have no control over how to do something or how well they will do, what is the point in trying? If students believe factors beyond their control determine their academic fortunes, why bother trying?

It is also important to recognize that a sense of control can be just as effective as actual control. This means that even if students are not in control of things now, if they believe that by trying hard and working effectively they can seize control, then that is good enough. Hence, students who have not yet got control but believe they can get it through good effort and strategy, behave as though they have got it. This is important to tell students who do not yet have the skill to perform to their potential, but with effective thought and action they can get there.

Disengagement and development

Another reason for disengagement relates to a student's developmental stage. As mentioned earlier, middle high school students (approximately 14–15 years of age) can find school a challenging part of their lives. They are experiencing substantial cognitive, social, physical, and emotional growth and development at this time – and school can have a tough time finding a place among this developmental activity. They are also striving for and receiving more autonomy than when they were younger. New friends, new liberties and new connections are all very seductive distractions from the perceived drudgery of school and schoolwork.

In some ways it may seem that schools and teachers (and parents) are powerless in the face of these quite monumental developmental challenges. In fact this is not the case. There are things schools and teachers can do to better engage students during the stress and storm of adolescence. Research has found that middle high students see their schoolwork as monotonous, unimportant, unconnected to their world and too repetitive. They also feel uninvolved in academic tasks and activities and believe they are in an academic wilderness – a long time since they began high school and a long time until they finish high school. Research has suggested that schools injecting importance, innovation, curiosity, novelty, purpose and inclusion into adolescents' academic lives are better placed to deal with potential developmental disengagement.

Modelling by parents and teachers

Students can also learn to be disengaged and helpless. Research has consistently demonstrated the powerful impact of modelling on children and young people. Students observe significant others and can learn to behave and respond similarly. Thus, if students see significant others respond in a helpless way, they may learn to be helpless as well. Early and powerful modelling occurs at home. Children whose parents behave in helpless and fearful ways or give up too easily may learn to operate in these problematic ways as well.

In addition to modelling, parents and significant others can also directly communicate their negative expectations to their children. Direct negative messages are those where parents and significant others tell children that they are not up to the job, are likely to perform poorly, or will do no good at school. Indirect negative messages are those where parents accept their children's poor performance without aspiring for better, express surprise if the children indicate an intention to go on to senior high, or are overheard telling relatives that the children are not cut out for school. Teachers can also provide direct and indirect messages that can lead to student disengagement. The examples noted above are heard and seen in classrooms the world over.

Problems at home might also be a source of disengagement. It is not unusual for an unhappy home life to get students down and this might generalize to school. It can be difficult to stay optimistic in one part of life when another part of life seems hopeless. Of course, an unhappy home life might also drive a student into the arms of school – time at school is much happier than time at home. Even in this case, however, schools would do well to remain vigilant. Research into youth resilience indicates that the presence of risk factors (e.g. trouble at home, poor parent–child relationships, family breakdown) can leave a child on a knife's edge – academic disengagement would be a sign that the risk factors are starting to bite.

Peer influence

The influence of peers can also be a cause of disengagement and helplessness. Students who start losing interest in school can drift to other students who are not switched on to school, or a student who begins to switch off may have a negative influence on other students in the group who have been travelling well. Sometimes, it does not take long before negative talk can cast a gloom over peers, particularly if the disengaged student happens to be a power broker in the group. In fact, sometimes a disengaged power broker in the class can have a negative effect on others in the class. Further, if negativity among peers goes unchecked there is a chance it can become something of a downward spiral, as it descends, it becomes harder to reverse.

Poor fit between student and teacher, class, or school

Disengagement may also occur because of a poor fit between the student and the teacher, poor fit between the student and the class, or in some cases poor fit between the student and the school. In the case of the first, sometimes a teacher is simply not suited to a student. Sometimes, personalities clash, the student presses the wrong buttons in a teacher, the student has difficulties the teacher is not equipped to deal with, the student's parents have clashed with the teacher, or the student and teacher may have a poor history from a previous year. In these cases, it is a good idea to try to work things through if at all possible – over the course of a long teaching career, there will be many such cases and if they keep leading to disengagement then that is not ideal. Indeed, this book concludes with a close look at ways to enhance teacher–student relationships in the classroom.

There may be a poor fit between student and class. Sometimes, students do not gel with their classmates, the class level of ability may be far too discrepant from the students' level of ability, the class is too raucous when the students are best suited to peace, or the class may be too quiet and orderly when the students are very active and demonstrative. Again, before hastily shifting the student, it would be prudent to try to make things work if possible – there is only so much shuffling of students a school can do before logistics get difficult to manage. Also, classrooms with a diverse mix of students can be energizing places to teach and learn.

Finally, there may be a poor fit between student and school. School ethos, school culture, school structure or school practices do not suit some students. There are many schools that do a good job of valuing and accepting all students, harnessing individual uniqueness and strengths, celebrating diversity, and making all students feel 'at home'. There are also occasions when in spite of doing all these things, some students just cannot seem to find their feet – through no fault of their own or the school's. Unfortunately, however, there are times when schools do not do a good job of accommodating students, leading to poor school-student fit and then to potential disengagement.

Mental health, bullying and social isolation

Research suggests that some disengaged students can pass through intense anger and anxiety in the early stages of helplessness and after a while this can lead to depression. Students' absolute conviction that there is nothing they can do to affect academic outcomes in their lives (e.g. to avoid failure or to attain success) can lead them to feel pretty miserable and abandon their sense of hope. The cycle of poor performance often feeds directly into extreme negativity and the joint operation of hopelessness and negativity can give rise to depression.

At this point, academic disengagement can hit new lows – lows that parents and teachers would never have thought possible. Once again, there is evidence of a vicious negative feedback loop where one problem compounds another. Indeed, it becomes difficult to disentangle cause and effect here – it seems poor mental health is causing disengagement and disengagement is exacerbating poor mental health.

It is at this point that students' mental health becomes more important than anything else – even their academic (dis)engagement. If students are depressed or experiencing anxiety or other problematic psychological conditions that are interfering with their functioning, they must receive help. Help can be sought from the school counsellor, school psychologist, GP, pediatrician, adolescent psychiatrist, local health clinic, university psychology clinic, community mental health unit, nearby hospital, or even a national or state psychological society or association for a referral.

A couple of other reasons students may disengage from school should also be mentioned, and which can also be related to mental health issues. They may be experiencing social problems at school. They may be feeling lonely or disconnected from others and this will not leave them feeling too great about other aspects of school, such as schoolwork and study. Another reason is that they may be being bullied at school. For a victim, bullying can turn school into a scary place and when school is a scary place, there is not so much room for effective engagement with schoolwork and study. Hence, these two problems can affect disengagement. Be prepared to talk with students very honestly and sensitively about these problems. Share your concerns about bullying with others in the school, ask what the school's policy is to deal with bullying and make sure they deploy this policy. Also ask students and their parents what you can do to support them during this difficult time.

Consequences of disengagement

Academic disengagement has academic consequences. It can also have non-academic consequences in students' lives now and well into their future. In my own research, academic consequences of disengagement include:

- less academic planning and more ineffective self-regulation
- greater academic anxiety
- lower academic self-esteem
- less persistence at school and in schoolwork
- less participation in class
- lower enjoyment of school
- negative educational aspirations
- lower academic resilience (an inability to bounce back from setback)

Other research has found academic disengagement and underachievement leads to:

- higher likelihood of school dropout
- increased absenteeism and school refusal
- chronic poor performance
- low educational attainment

There are also negative non-academic consequences of academic disengagement and underachievement including:

- negative peer affiliation (mixing with the wrong crowd)
- increased likelihood of unemployment through the lifespan compared with students who achieve
- relatively low salary compared with students who achieved at school

- increased risk of 'churn' in the labour market (in and out of jobs, patchy employment)
- low general self-esteem
- poor mental health
- poor life resilience

Research suggests that more than any other type of student, those who are disengaged from school and schoolwork reflect some of the most problematic academic and non-academic outcomes. Also important to note is that these consequences are not confined to school and the academic lifespan. They extend into early adulthood and beyond.

Equally worrying, research shows that there can be generational disengagement, helplessness and underachievement; that is, children are more likely to underachieve if their parents were underachieving, disaffected and disengaged when at school. Thus, there is a potential generational cost following an inability to engage students and have them achieve to personal potential.

Certainly, some highly successful people were disengaged and underachieving at school. It is therefore important not to assume that disengagement is an intractable life sentence. Having said this, however, research clearly shows that successful pathways are less likely than problematic pathways and so it is imperative that disengagement is tackled as soon and as robustly as possible.

Conclusion

Although disengagement and helplessness apply to a relative minority of students, there are few things more frustrating (and soul destroying) to parents and teachers than a student who has disengaged from school. Perhaps more than any other students, those who have disengaged reflect the downside of the '80/20 rule': 80 per cent of students take 20 per cent of a school's time and resources while 20 per cent of students can take 80 per cent of time and resources. This 20 per cent comprises many disengaged students. Thus, for both student and school alike, it is important to intervene.

Factors relevant to academic disengagement include a low sense of control, poor fit between student and school, developmental potholes, learning difficulties, chronic poor performance, poor modelling by parents or teachers, trouble in a student's personal life, and difficulties in a student's interpersonal life.

Disengaged students are the consequence of ineffectively addressing fear and failure early. They are at the end of a slippery fear and failure slope. Unsuccessful efforts to redress overstriving, defensive pessimism, success avoidance and self-handicapping can lead to disengagement and helplessness. Heading off these early fear and failure indicators goes a long way to heading off disengagement. Part 4 suggests many strategies teachers can use to do just this.

8

OVERSTRIVING AND PERFECTIONISM

It is a lot of pressure for me to get to uni ... To get to university is more pressure than anything, because I think it is a matter of life and death. And once I get into it, I have to keep on being successful.

Dominique, age 17

[My father] wants me to do the best that I can, but my best isn't good enough ... Dad's a bit, 'I expect more from my daughter, we expect you not to shame us or the community'. It's a shame I couldn't be a doctor. That was his goal for me. To be a doctor. I have all this on my shoulders.

Mia, age 17

There are many students who live in fear of failure and work obsessively to avoid it. This type of student is called an overstriver. Overstrivers avoid failure by succeeding. They do this not so much by focusing on success, but by focusing on failure and dedicating themselves to avoiding it. They are therefore focused more on failure than success. Because overstrivers focus on failure, they tend to be fearful, always looking over their shoulder at the wolves snapping at their heels.

This type of student represents a relatively large proportion of the student body. Particularly in high school – and then more so in senior high school when the heat of the competitive blow torch is really turned up – failure and fear of it looms large in these students' minds. As the heat is turned up, so are fear and the desire to avoid poor performance. Some students deal with this through self-handicapping, defensive pessimism and disengagement. However, there are others that deal with this through turning up the heat on themselves and this typically takes the form of excessive study, excessive diligence, and obsessive attention to assessment and evaluation tasks. These students are referred to as overstrivers.

Chloe is a prime example. She works extremely hard in class, is intent on writing the most perfect essays and assignments possible, and studies over and above most other students. However, what drives this high level of application is uncertainty in her ability and her fear of performing poorly. Thus, she does not so much study to succeed; instead, she studies mainly to avoid performing poorly. This is not much of a problem while she performs well. However, it does become a problem when she receives a result that is lower than she expected. In her mind, this confirms her self-doubt. Moreover, any more 'bad' results and she may seek more self-defeating ways to deal with her fear of failure or poor performance – self-handicapping, defensive pessimism and disengagement are three such ways.

Ways to recognize an overstriver

Overstrivers are driven. They are driven to avoid failure, driven to avoid missing out on a university place, driven to gain others' approval, driven to prove themselves, driven to avoid mistakes, driven to top the class, and driven to know more than others. In being driven, overstrivers are never quite satisfied with where they are.

What is the alternative? Understanding the difference between being 'driven' and being 'drawn' is a useful way of looking at alternative motivations. This alternative involves students being drawn to success, drawn to personal improvement, drawn to learning and understanding new things, drawn to curiosity, drawn to courses at university that interest them, drawn to participation and cooperation, drawn to solving problems, and drawn to doing a good job for its own sake and not just for marks. For these students, fear and failure are not top-of-mind. Instead, they focus on positive and adaptive outcomes and processes, and are drawn to these. As a result, they tend to enjoy school more than the overstrivers.

Another feature of overstrivers is that they always seem to be trying to prove themselves to others or to themselves. They seem to be on a constant quest to prove they are competent or prove they are not incompetent, prove they are better or prove that they are not worse, and prove they know more or prove they do not know less. Sadly, this is a never-ending pursuit. There is always someone else to prove oneself to. Because of this, overstrivers are rarely satisfied with where they are at any point in time.

Because they need to prove themselves and because they invest a great deal of their self-worth in proving themselves, overstrivers also feel the need to over-perform. An A grade is not satisfying, if an A+ was possible. Performing in the top 10 per cent is not acceptable if there is a top 5 per cent band identified.

Indeed, here we are getting very close to perfectionism, which is discussed below.

To the extent that overstrivers are never quite as satisfied with good performance as they should be, they are excessively dissatisfied with poor performance to the point of distress. They tend to dwell on poor performance more than good performance, they tend to dwell on past poor grades more than they look forward to good grades, they tend to berate themselves for bad results and do not take enough credit or satisfaction in good results. As described below, this is a risky cut-point for overstrivers. If self-doubt builds to a point of pessimism or to a point where they believe poor performance is likely, they run the risk of moving to a more self-defeating way of dealing with their fear; again, self-handicapping, defensive pessimism and disengagement are three such ways.

Overstrivers also tend to be overly competitive, but are too easily spooked by competition and their competitors if things do not go well. Competition and competiveness are great while things are going the student's way. But what about when things do not go the student's way? Overstrivers can come unstuck at this point. Thoughts of inadequacy can start to dominate. Again, this can be a risky cut-point – if self-doubt and pessimism start to take hold, the overstriver may reach for more self-defeating ways to deal with fear and failure.

Success is possible without overstriving

The point of the above discussion is not to imply that hard work, diligence and preparation are not good things. Quite the contrary; these factors are the cornerstones of students' success. They should be prized, celebrated and lauded. The problem with overstrivers is that they take these things to the extreme and compound them with fear. Such unbalanced diligence that is motivated by fear is not needed to perform well.

It is also important to recognize that focusing on success is another way to attain success. The overstriver attains success by focusing on and avoiding failure. With fear and failure ever present in their mind, is it any wonder they tend to be anxious and high in self-doubt? Swinging the focus towards success and how to attain it reduces negative thoughts, feelings and motivations, and increases optimism and positive motivations and engagement. In so doing, it is possible to succeed without being an overstriver.

Causes of overstriving

A big part of overstriving is bound up in self-worth. Overstrivers pin a lot of their self-worth on how well they do. As described at the start of this book, when a student's self-worth is overly invested in their academic performance, there is a lot at stake. There are very good reasons to fear failure and be motivated to avoid it. Overstriving is a strategy students can use to avoid poor performance and keep self-worth intact.

It is possible that approval at home is also meted out on the basis of academic performance. Approval from parents is so important to students (even though they may deny it) that this can be another factor driving their need to avoid failure. Moreover, they may be celebrated at home for the good results they achieve and this brings with it a greater motivation to avoid the loss of this approval. Related to this, children may be punished for not achieving results to their parents' satisfaction and this can also put in place a failure-avoidant orientation. According to Mia, 'I can't eat the night before an exam. All night I have nightmares that I'm going to fail and that Dad's going to come after me'. Similar dynamics can occur at school, where students are valued more highly if they achieve academically and devalued or punished if they do not.

Following from this, parents may invest their own worth in their child's academic achievement – clearly taking more than a measured pleasure in their child's results. Boasting to friends and relatives about their child's academic performance runs the risk of turning up failure-avoidant pressure on the child. Likewise, displaying shame and embarrassment following poor results can sow the seeds of fear and failure. Again, similar dynamics can occur at school with teachers clearly investing too much of their own worth in their students' achievement, and clearly taking it too personally when students do not achieve.

Expanding on the above two points, it is also possible that an overstriving school (or classroom) ethos or culture can develop. Some achieving schools or classrooms can be characterized by fear and fear dynamics. In these schools and classrooms, students achieve because they are frightened of not achieving. There are subtle and not so subtle messages telling students that to fail is to let the school or class down. In these schools and classrooms, the focus is on avoiding failure, not striving for success.

Finally, it must be recognized that temperament and personality are also factors in overstriving. There are some students who are apprehensive by nature; that is who they are and they have always been like it. Given this, there is a need to be sensitive and realistic when dealing with problematic behaviour if there is a dispositional basis for it. Here efforts are not so much directed at changing the person, but changing behaviours and attitudes that might be getting in the way of a student's achievement motivation. Part 4 details many ways this can be done.

Consequences of overstriving

Looking first at the upside of overstriving, it must be acknowledged that many overstrivers succeed academically. Many a school dux has been an overstriver. It is no accident that when students invest vast amounts of time, effort and energy into schoolwork, they have a good chance of academic success. Indeed, this is the very seductive aspect of overstriving – it comes with a tangible upside. In fact, many parents and teachers will compliment the student for such diligence, and in some respects, who can blame them? Academic diligence makes life a lot easier at home and in the classroom.

So what's the problem? Effort, diligence and achievement are pretty hard to argue with.

The problem – or the potential problem – relates to other aspects of academic life. Because overstrivers are very focused on failure and avoiding it, their top-of-mind focus tends to be a negative and fearful one. When students' school life is characterized by negativity and fear, their day-to-day experience is not a particularly pleasant one – at least, it is not as pleasant as it could be. According to Olivia, age 17, 'Assignments are a perpetual stressing thing for me. When they're due, I get really nervous and I always think that for some reason I'm off track, when I'm really on track ... I put more stress on myself'.

School can also become a bit of a roller coaster. Up for a while, but then worrying and feeling negative about the next test, quiz, exam or assignment. Typically, overstrivers feel more relief than happiness at a good result and so even their highs are not as high or long as they should be. When students' emotions are pushed and pulled like this on an ongoing basis (and it is ongoing because evaluation and assessment are a constant feature of school life), school becomes a place of instability rather than stability, angst rather than peace.

It must also be remembered that childhood and youth is a special time of life and a time to be enjoyed as much as possible. Overstrivers often lack the balance in life needed to enjoy pursuits other than study. Because they over-prepare and over-invest, they are not likely to be the students having an idle or fun Sunday afternoon. With the wolves snapping at their heels, there is no time to waste.

Extending this a little further, they may also lack the down time necessary for mental and physical health. Many an overstriver has burnt themselves out, worked to the point of exhaustion, run out of puff when it really mattered. School is a long haul. Students need to pace themselves and recharge and re-energize at key times.

Finally, the overstriving student is not particularly resilient or mentally tough. Because they live in constant self-doubt, any setback, failure, mistake or loss can confirm the doubts they have about themselves and they are then at risk of reaching for a more self-defeating way of dealing with failure – self-handicapping and defensive pessimism are two such ways. Thus, if overstriving does serve its function (avoid failure by succeeding), then in the medium to longer term, more problematic behaviours and thinking might set in.

Perfectionism

The perfectionist is very similar to the overstriver. As the name suggests, perfectionists aim to do things perfectly. Perfectionists are included in this book because they tie a lot of their self-worth and self-esteem to their ability to do things perfectly. Anything less than perfect is seen as a 'failure' and a threat to their self-esteem and worth as a person. 'Failure', then, is to be avoided at all cost because it is a direct threat to the student's worth. Perfectionism, therefore, is founded on fear. This is compounded by the fact that perfectionists often receive a lot of praise and approval for doing things perfectly and doing anything less than perfect risks a loss of approval from others.

As with the overstriver, the upside of perfectionism can be success. Students who invest effort, energy and diligence are often rewarded with academic achievement. However, for the perfectionist, success can become something of a shackle; it becomes the minimum standard. This has two implications. First, attaining minimum standards is not exactly satisfying. Thus, success has less capacity to satisfy the perfectionist. Second, by having such a high minimum standard, there is a heightened risk of 'failure'. Similar to the overstriver, if failure looms large in perfectionists' minds and perfectionism has not been effective in avoiding it, then more self-defeating behaviours may ensue. In fact, some perfectionists eventually decide they would rather not run the race at all than run the race and 'lose'.

There are other downsides to perfectionism. The perfectionist's journey is often not a pleasant one, characterized by anxiety, fear and tension. Also, their life is often not a balanced one. They can spend inordinate amounts of time trying to perfect something at the expense of doing other important things in life. Moreover, there are many perfectionists who do not get a great deal done. They can spend an entire week or weekend working on an assignment only to give up near the deadline because it is not going to be a perfect job or neglect other schoolwork while they are doing the assignment.

It is again important to note that effort and diligence are not the problem here. Rather, it is the extremes of effort and diligence coupled with the fear factor that become problems for perfectionists. What we might recommend for perfectionists is to shoot for excellence rather than perfection – and in the process, take pride in excellence and learn to live a little.

Success seeking

So, what is the alternative to overstriving and perfectionism? In short, success seeking. As detailed at the outset of this book, success seekers are students who are focused on achieving success (rather than avoiding failure), optimistic, self-assured, low in self-doubt and proactively forward-looking. Do success seekers always succeed? No. They are not strangers to failure. However, what distinguishes them from the overstriver is that they have a very different response to their failings. They take the lesson to be learnt and move on. In fact, some of them even see their failures as opportunities to improve next time. They see mistakes as the windows to future success. In contrast to overstrivers who obsess and berate themselves for failing, success seekers are on the front foot and ready to embrace the next challenge – not shrink from it.

It seems, then, that it is often the reason students do things that determine whether they are an overstriver or a success seeker. Encouraging students to do things primarily for avoidance reasons can determine whether they are overstrivers or success seekers. For example, promoting a fear of not getting into university as the only reason to do any study is likely to set a student up as an overstriver. On the other hand, encouraging improvement, personal bests (PBs), skill development, learning and skill development as reasons to study is likely to set up a success seeker. More is said about this in Part 4.

Research has shed quite a lot of light on the reasons students have for doing what they do. It seems that people can invest serious effort and energy without being exhausted if they have positive reasons for doing what they do. On the other hand, when people invest lots of effort and energy for negative and fear-based reasons, we find they run out of steam and can be depleted over the medium to longer term. Hence, students who work hard at school and study because they are striving to improve, develop and work to personal potential tend to be energized through the process. On the other hand, students who work hard because they are frightened of failing, do not want to get into trouble, or do not want to disappoint parents or teachers are not fuelled by positive energy. As a result, they can deteriorate through the process.

Conclusion

Success can be a way to avoid failure. Overstrivers avoid failure by succeeding. However, because overstrivers focus on failure, they tend to be fearful, always looking over their shoulder at the wolves snapping at their heels. The central problem for overstrivers is that they are motivated by a fear of failure and confound their diligence with fear. Thus, they are driven by failure rather than drawn to success.

Overstrivers tie their self-worth onto how well they do. When a student's self-worth is overly invested in academic performance, there is a lot at stake and there are very real reasons to fear failure and be motivated to avoid it. Overstriving is a strategy students can use to avoid poor performance and keep self-worth intact.

Although success can be an upside to overstriving, there are also numerous potential costs to the student. Self-doubt, pressure, low or non-existent levels of satisfaction, fear, and the possibility of low resilience can become part of the frame. Because of this, there is merit in seeking other ways to attain success.

Focusing on success is one such way. Swinging the focus towards success and how to attain it reduces negative thoughts, feelings and motivations – and increases optimism and positive motivations and engagement. In so doing, it is possible to succeed without being an overstriver.

Students who manage to do this are referred to as success seekers. Success seekers are students who are focused on achieving success (rather than avoiding failure), optimistic, self-assured (and low in self-doubt), forward-looking, and unlikely to dwell on shortcomings or failings. If they do not perform well, they take the lesson to be learnt and move on; thus, they remain upbeat, optimistic and resilient in the face of setback.

9

FEAR OF SUCCESS AND SUCCESS AVOIDANCE

If you get a good mark, they'll expect you to do the same thing again.

Gwen, age 15

Believe it or not, avoiding success can be a way to avoid failure – at least, a particular type of failure. It is also a self-defeating way to deal with fear. But why would someone want to avoid success? Why would someone fear it? This seems quite counter-intuitive; particularly given the chapters thus far seem to imply that a lack of success drives fear and failure avoidance.

There are four types of success avoiders/fearers:

1. Students who do not want to do well because they will look different or stand out from the group.
2. Students who do not want to do well because they will incur friends' or the group's disapproval or disappointment.
3. Students who do not want to do well because there will be more pressure on them to do well next time.
4. Students who believe they do not deserve their success and fear further success because that moves them one step closer to being 'found out'.

As detailed below, in each case fear is a prime motivator. Moreover, in different ways, failure is also a prime motivator. In fact, after a while, students who back away from success opportunities find themselves faced with a new set of problems – problems involving failure.

In some ways, the success fearer and the success avoider are easier to deal with than the other problematic students discussed in this book. At least for these students success is not far away. The main challenge with these students is to address some of their problematic beliefs that is driving their aversion to success. The challenge for other problematic students is not only to address problematic beliefs but also move them away from entrenched failure dynamics to get within the realm of possible success.

Standing out from the crowd

As indicated above, one reason students do not want to do so well at school is because they do not want to look different or stand out from the group. For some students in some groups, standing out from the pack is not a good thing. It can lead to teasing, ridicule and self-consciousness. Young people hate being teased and ridiculed and many certainly also hate feeling self-conscious. Although adolescence is often seen as a rebellious stage in life, it is also a stage when conforming to the peer group is a high priority. To stand out from the peer group risks disapproval, one's place in the group, and one's respect from group members.

Students who do well and are in groups or environments where this is not valued run the risk of being singled out for 'special' treatment from peers; therefore, it is not uncommon for students to fly under the radar by not performing so well that they draw attention to themselves in threatening ways; that is, they do not perform to their potential and in doing so, avoid success. The failure they are trying to avoid here is social or peer failure. To stand out from the crowd in a bad way is a form of social or peer failure. Thus, in a different sort of way, success avoidance is a form of failure avoidance.

It is also evident that fear drives the success avoider. Fear of looking different, fear of being noticed in an unhelpful way, fear of incurring peers' disapproval, fear of being seen to be a 'nerd' – essentially, fear of success.

They will also be the type of student who does not want public recognition for success. In the face of peer pressure, there will be some students who perform well but do not want this to be noted in the public domain. They will shrink from awards, certificates, lists of class ranks on the notice board and honour rolls. They are at pains to keep their achievements to themselves; thus, although not success avoiders, they are certainly success fearers.

It should also be noted that boys are more likely than girls to be this type of success avoider (but of course there are many girls who are this type as well). Boys can be very fearful of standing out from the pack. Boys tend to be more overt and punishing about those who look different (but girls have their ways to punish as well). Boys are also more uncomfortable receiving academic awards and accolades. It tends to be the boys who would rather an academic certificate was quietly slipped into their hands than handed to them in front of the school.

Age can also make a difference. Primary (or elementary) school students tend to be more comfortable with achievement and recognition of achievement. It is the high school students that have more of a problem with it, particularly those in the middle high years (e.g. 14–15 years). This is a shame because poor habits that develop here can really bite in senior high school when it can be harder to turn things around.

> Neal, age 14, is a good example. Neal is a bright boy, capable of high achievement in all school subjects, did well in primary school and at the beginning of high school, but has hit middle high school and has dipped in achievement. He would not be categorized as disengaged or an underachiever; rather, his performance has just come off the boil so that now he is more of a mid-range performer – now top 30 per cent and no longer top 10 per cent. It turns out that a culture in the classroom had developed in which students getting very good marks were finding 'L' (for 'loser') graffiti on their school books. This upset Neal immensely and also made him feel a bit frightened of other possible retribution. In his mind, the good marks were the problem, not the bullies, and that is when the achievement dips set in.

As detailed in Part 4, it takes courage to succeed and specific strategies to build this courage is addressed.

Incurring disapproval

Another reason students back away from possible success is because they do not want to incur the disapproval of friends. Particularly in high school, there are peer groups where everyone has their place and it is important not to upset the group dynamics or the rules of the circle. These rules can include codes of fashion, turn-taking, decision-making, who is in the group and who is out of the group, where the group sits at lunchtime, and other students or groups allowed to be friends.

Of relevance to the themes in this book, there can also be rules around academic performance and what agreed-on pecking order is around performance. For example, in some groups a particular student is known as the achiever; or, an entire group defines itself in terms of a certain level of academic achievement. All is well and good when success fits the group norms and rules. However, there are times when academic success exceeds the group norms or breaks the group's rules. The offending student is likely to then incur disapproval from peers in the group. Because disapproval is not a pleasant thing to experience from one's peers (particularly during the high school years), some students opt to keep performance relatively lower to stay in good with the group.

Just as a fear of looking different is more likely to haunt boys, fear of breaking the rules of the circle or the friendship dynamics tends to be greater among girls (but many boys can also be troubled by this fear as well). Thus, fear of success and success avoidance seem to be more embedded in interrelationships and interrelationship dynamics for girls (though there is obviously a relatedness component to boys' fear and avoidance as well).

Katarina, age 14, is a new girl at the local high school, her family having just moved to the area. She falls on her feet with a new set of friends 'adopting' her and giving her a great sense of belonging and inclusion at the new school. She is not unused to learning the various interpersonal dynamics that are needed to get on in friendship circles and is keen to figure out as best possible what is involved in this new group of friends. Most of the group rules sit comfortably with her – nothing out of the ordinary and nothing too challenging – except for one. The group is a relatively high achieving one and is presided over by a girl (Robyn, age 14) who consistently outperforms the other group members. For Katarina, who is also a high achiever, this poses a challenge. To stay in with the girls and not fall out of favour, she must quite carefully manage her achievement so as not to outperform Robyn. For the most part, this is not a major problem because Robyn really does excel. But what it means is that whenever Katarina asks herself if she should go the extra mile to really strive for a top mark, she decides not to. Thus, she has the potential for excellence if she digs in hard, but usually opts for less than this. Relative to her potential, then, Katarina is a success avoider and overly influenced by fear of success and the potential disapproval this will incur.

Pressure to do well next time

Some students do not want to do too well because there is more pressure on them to do well down the track. Some students do not want to achieve highly because their parents raise the bar to a level that the student is not comfortable with. Some students do not want to perform highly at school because they are uncomfortable with the high expectations teachers then put on them. Some students do not want to be known as a top performer because the pressure of being school dux or top of the class is too great.

For these students, the weight of expectation and aspiration is too great a burden. Every time they succeed, significant others in their lives roll out the pressure and expectation and these students find this aversive. Every time a good report card comes home, there is renewed talk of a top-level course at a top-level university and this only adds to the pressure.

One way to deal with this is to report as little good news at home as possible. However, positive feedback inevitably makes it home via formal school communication such as newsletters, report cards or contact with teachers. Also, this does not get around pressure from teachers and school to excel, so this way of dealing with the burden of success is not entirely effective.

A surer way to ease the weight of expectation is to slip into a more comfortable zone of achievement. Slipping down a few rungs to be in the top ten rather than the top three students keeps one out of the firing line. Certainly, people are nagging the student to do better, but for this student the nagging is far preferable to the pressure to top the year group or gain entry to an elite university. It is therefore no surprise to find many extremely capable students never quite performing to their potential and not being overly concerned about this.

Looking closely at these students, it is evident that both fear and failure play a part in all this. They fear not being able to sustain achievement to a level that is required to hit the top and they fear the consequences of this for their self-worth. Failing to meet goals is potentially damaging to one's self-worth. It will be recalled the defensive optimists set goals they have no hope of reaching and so can blame the goal rather than their lack of ability. For the high achiever, failing to meet high goals or standards is very different. They see it as genuine failure because there was a chance they could have succeeded, and they did not. When faced with this prospect, some students opt for a lower-achieving comfort zone and in so doing are opting to avoid success.

Tom, age 16, is tired of his parents pushing him to Medicine, the university pathway requiring the highest marks for entry, and by implication the most competitive to get into. His parents believe that Tom should do the highest possible university course that his marks entitle him to. Tom is one of the best students at his school, but getting the marks for Medicine is a big push for him. He is not a very confident student, he is never quite sure that he fully deserves his marks, and the effect of both these is that he fears he cannot keep up the good grades to get into Medicine. One option is to pull back a bit and put Medicine out of range. If Tom adopts this strategy, fear and failure will have been the key driving forces in his decision to avoid success.

The Impostor Syndrome

There is another fear related to success that deserves special mention: fear of being exposed as a fraud. There are many students who achieve and perform highly but who believe that one day they will be exposed as people who are actually not competent or capable. This is known as the Impostor Syndrome. It refers to a belief that one is incompetent and masquerading as someone who is competent. For this student, every success is just one step closer to being found out; every success further embroils the student in the fraud. It is for this reason that success is feared so intensely by the 'impostor' and many actually avoid success for this reason.

Marcia, age 16, excels at school. Unfortunately, she does not enjoy her success and she hates people praising her or hearing positive feedback on her schoolwork. She also feels very anxious whenever someone compliments her excellent grades and feels deeply uncomfortable whenever her talents are showcased at home, in class or in front of the school. The reality is that Marcia, despite her quite consistent success, does not fundamentally believe she is good at school or particularly clever. In fact, she genuinely believes that she has managed to fool the world and fears that one day she will take a dramatic fall from grace when she is exposed as incompetent. She believes she is an impostor and the more she succeeds, the greater her fall when it comes. Her fear-based impostor beliefs lead to her feeling anxious and do not allow her to enjoy her success. The other downside to these beliefs is that they can erode her resilience. Because she doubts her abilities, setback will confirm those doubts. When doubt begins to overwhelm her, she is at risk of unravelling in ways that lead to problematic behaviours.

Factors that shape avoidance and fear of success

Although many factors have the potential to shape students' fear of success or success avoidance, three are key:

- low self-esteem
- self-esteem that is based on unhelpful foundations
- uncertainty about the reasons for success

Low self-esteem underpins the reasons why Neal does not want to distinguish himself from the crowd, Katarina is influenced by her friends' approval, Tom does not want to aim as high as he can, and Marcia constantly doubts herself. If students do not have the self-belief to back themselves in the face of detractors, then they will short-change themselves academically. If students do not have the confidence to stand on their own, then they will not rise above the norm. Self-esteem is a basis for achieving to one's potential and being able to withstand some ribbing from peers. Self-esteem is a basis for aiming high even if there is a chance it will not pay off. Self-esteem is a basis for recognizing that success is usually no accident and that one is usually entitled to it. Essentially, self-esteem is a basis for success seeking not success avoidance.

Students can also get into difficulty if they pin their self-esteem to unhelpful foundations. For example, Katarina pinned her self-esteem to her friends' approval. Because this was the basis of her self-worth, she was unduly driven by it. Accordingly, she regulated her academic effort so as not to risk disapproval and consequent self-esteem. Neal pinned his self-esteem to his ability to conform to the group and not stand out from the pack in any way. Thus, conformity became the factor determining his academic application because to fail at this would mean a blow to his self-esteem. To some extent, Tom's self-esteem was tied to his ability to attain high expectations set by significant others. Because he was unsure if he could attain these high expectations and because a failure to do so would risk his self-esteem, lower-range options were considered attractive. Reducing the links between self-esteem and problematic foundations (such as peer approval) is a way of significantly reducing fear and avoidance of academic success.

Looking closely at the above examples, it is also evident that a great deal of uncertainty resides in these students' minds. They are uncertain if they have what it takes, uncertain of their place in a group, uncertain if they can meet expectations, and uncertain if they are deserving of success. When such uncertainties exist, it is no wonder that students may manoeuvre in ways to protect themselves, even if it means achieving below their potential.

Moreover, when uncertainty is combined with low self-esteem, it can make for quite a lethal motivation cocktail: the student concludes that they cannot and should not strive for success and so begins a process of self-defeating behaviour. This combination of uncertainty and low self-esteem becomes a real barrier. Indeed, quite the opposite pattern is demonstrated in the case of high self-esteem: when students high in self-esteem are faced with uncertainty, they back themselves and go for it. Moreover, if they hit setback, they are not bluffed by it. Because they are high in self-esteem, they take the lesson to be learnt, apply it, and move onwards and upwards.

Conclusion

In a book dedicated to preventing fear and failure in the classroom, it may at first be surprising to see a chapter focusing on success. However, when success is seen as something of a double-edged sword – great for some students, but something very different for others – we go some way to understanding it as something that can excite or frighten students. For students whose self-esteem is shaky, based on problematic foundations and compounded by uncertainty in the academic setting, success can take a potentially frightening form.

Students who see a dark side to success tend to be those for whom success represents something of a failure. It may be a failure to fit in. It may be a failure to gain approval. It may be a failure to achieve to high expectations. In other cases, success may represent more of a fear than a failure; for example, a fear that greater success means a greater fall when it comes.

In such instances, fear of success and success avoidance become as much an academic barrier as the other self-defeating behaviours and orientations addressed in this book. At the heart of success avoidance lie fear and quite diverse forms of failure. Although these forms are not always academically based (e.g. it might be social failure the student is trying to avoid), they can have negative academic consequences. Accordingly, the strategies detailed in Part 4 are also directed at students' problematic orientations to success.

PART 4

BUILDING CLASSROOM SUCCESS, ELIMINATING ACADEMIC FEAR AND FAILURE

10

COURAGEOUS AND CONSTRUCTIVE VIEWS OF POOR PERFORMANCE

Failing means you're a loser.

Kurt, age 17

Kurt sums up the bottom-line belief that gets in the way of success. Failure and poor performance can hit students' self-esteem so hard that their main aim is to protect themselves rather than succeed.

What will be shown in this chapter is that failure and poor performance can be critical building blocks for later success. The people that rise in the face of adversity, challenge and possible poor performance know this fundamental truth. When Kurt learns that failure or poor performance does not mean he is a loser, he will have made the first (and perhaps most important) step on the way to success.

This chapter is aimed at tackling head on the way students think about failure. It is their beliefs about failure that can get them into difficulty. It is these beliefs that motivate them to engage in self-defeating protective behaviour.

Different reactions to failure or poor performance

The way students view failure or poor performance affects their behaviour, particularly their tendency to engage in problematic academic behaviour.

Every student has failed or performed poorly at some stage in their lives. But why do some fall in a heap after failing while others learn from their adversity and seem to use it to their advantage next time? Why are some students terrified to fail while others are not? Why are some students dominated by the fear of failure and poor performance, while others focus on how they can succeed following poor performance? The reasons for two such totally different reactions to failure or poor performance are the beliefs that students hold about failure and what they think failure says about them.

Failure and poor performance are not the be all and end all

The first reason many students are crushed by failure is because they see failure or poor performance as the be all and end all. They are crushed by failure or poor performance because they see failure or poor performance as judge, jury and executioner for their self-esteem and self-worth. It means they are failures, they are losers, and that is all there is to it. According to them, there is no other purpose for failure other than telling them they are hopeless.

Importantly, other students are not bluffed by failure. This is because they see failure as part of the learning process. They see failure or poor performance as valuable feedback on how to improve their next performance. These students do not focus on failure or poor performance as the outcomes; rather, they see them as part of a process and are skilled at taking from their poor performance what is needed for the next performance.

When failure and poor performance are viewed as the ingredients for later success, they do not overwhelm students. When students shift the focus away from their poor performance and onto how their performance can be improved next time, they are not threatened by the possibility of poor performance. For example, the best students take what they need from failure or poor performance and put it into practice in the very next study session or exam. The very best students are keen to know what they did not know in the exam and are even keener to know it next time round.

The first Teacher Tip, then, is to help students see poor performance as providing the secrets to achieve later improvement and success. When students view poor performance in this way, they do not live in abject fear of performing poorly. Instead, they view it much more positively. When viewed in this way, these students are unlikely to be motivated to protect their self-esteem. This is because improvement and then success become the focus and not self-esteem protection.

Teacher Tip 1

Show students how failure and poor performance can provide important information about how they can do better next time

---

Failure or poor performance are not necessarily an indication of incompetence

Another reason why some students are devastated by failure and poor performance is because they believe that failure or poor performance means that they are incompetent or are not clever.

This is quickly followed by the belief that they must not be worthwhile people. For many students, then, failure or poor performance mean that they are fundamentally incapable and they then conclude that they are low in worth. When failure and poor performance are viewed in this way, how can they not devastate students? Of course these students would feel a sense of hopelessness when they believe that failure or poor performance mean that they are fundamentally incapable. Students who think this way are particularly drawn to self-defeating protective behaviour.

On the other hand, other students believe that failure or poor performance say a lot about their strategies, their knowledge and how hard they try. When they fail, these students work on refining or improving the way they do things, gaining the knowledge required for better performance, and trying harder. So, in stark contrast to being devastated by and shrinking from failure or poor performance, these students take very positive steps to take what they need out of their failure or poor performance and apply it next time round. More importantly, they know that there usually is a 'next time' and focus on that rather than the 'last time'; that is, through their belief that failure and poor performance reflect on things they can do something about rather than reflecting on a fundamental incompetence, these students are energized following failure and poor perfor-mance, not overcome by them.

This leads to the next Teacher Tip that states that poor performance says a lot about how hard students try, the way they do things, and the knowledge they have. Hence, the good news is that students can improve.

Teacher Tip 2

Help students understand that failure and poor performance say a lot about how hard they try, the way they do things, and their knowledge – and these can be improved

---

Sometimes students' standards are way too tough

Some students are destroyed by failure or poor performance because of the tough personal standards they have set that tell them they have failed or performed poorly. One student who, in the state-wide final exams, received the second highest mark in the school and was easily in the top 0.1 per cent of the state. As it turned out, this was a great source of shame to her because she did not top the school. While most other students would have been thrilled with the result, as far as she was concerned, she had failed.

Essentially, then, some students can be too hard on themselves when they set their standards for success and failure. It is therefore suggested that students set challenging but realistic success zones for themselves. A 'success zone' refers to the range of performance that students decide will indicate success. The student just mentioned set herself up for failure because she did not set a constructive success zone. Rather, her definition of success was too tough and almost guaranteed personal failure. The tougher students' success zones are, the more they run the risk of personal failure. Thus, students must be somewhat flexible in their idea of what to expect of themselves in upcoming performances.

Now, some will rightly point out that the best athletes in the world or the most successful businesspeople have got to the top because they aimed to be number one and that if they had not set such a restrictive standard they would never have got there. The point here is that these restrictive standards of absolute excellence might be feasible for the top handful in any given field but what about the rest of us mere mortals? If the advice here was to set sights at being the best in the world, then this instantly relegates most students to failure because only one individual can be the top of any given field. Importantly, however, the advice here is not restricting students to mediocrity. Rather, it is important to encourage students to develop realistic but challenging success zones; then, with each good performance, aim to push students' success zones a little further. Each time students push them a little further, they reach new personal bests (PBs). One day they will look back at where they were earlier and be amazed to see that all these smaller gains have added up to a very substantial gain overall.

This brings us to the third Teacher Tip. With every new challenge, set realistic but challenging standards to meet.

Teacher Tip 3
Set challenging but realistic 'success zones' (the range of performance that indicates success) for upcoming schoolwork; then, with each success, set students' success zone a little higher

Students' beliefs about what defines success and failure

Another reason why failure or poor performance hit some students harder than others is because of their narrow view of what success and failure say about them. In university life, I have submitted many academic papers for publication in prestigious academic journals. Early in my career, I was hammered by editors and reviewers who criticized my thinking, my writing style, my data analysis or my interpretation of results. Needless to say, in a number of cases, they whole-heartedly rejected my papers. My view of success and failure at that time was whether my paper got accepted or not. Not surprisingly, I was pretty down whenever my papers were rejected.

After a while I expanded my view of success to incorporate other significant gains I had made. First, it was significant that I had given it a go. Second, I learnt to give myself credit for designing a questionnaire, collecting data, reviewing a lot of complex research, and coming to some useful conclusions. Certainly, one journal I sent it to did not like it, but I could deal with the editor's concerns and submit it to another reputable journal. Thus, while I had not been accepted by the first journal, I had actually chalked up a number of other successes.

This brings us to the fourth Teacher Tip that states that students need to recognize the 'process' gains they make in their lives. Sometimes it will appear that they have performed poorly and they will feel like failures. This is because they have focused solely on 'product' gains (e.g. marks, rank). But if these students look more closely at their performance, they will see that there is often evidence of process successes. These include improvement, PBs, skill development, gains in knowledge and new under-standings. Admittedly, I had failed to get my article published in the first journal I had submitted it to, but I also succeeded in a number of other ways. When I shifted the focus onto these process gains, I was not so deflated by rejection.

Teacher Tip 4

Encourage students to expand their view of success to include the process gains (e.g. improvement, PBs, skill development, new understanding) they make in their academic lives

---

Conclusion

It is suggested that students need to think differently about failure or poor performance. As the previous chapters have shown, the reason they need to think differently about failure or poor performance is because their beliefs about failure or poor performance motivate them to self-protect in problematic ways. It is the beliefs about failure or poor performance that separate those students who dread the next challenge from those students who eagerly await it. Often, it is the beliefs about failure or poor performance that separate those students who are overwhelmed by poor performance from those who then go on to succeed.

By changing students' beliefs about failure and success and what they mean, students are not engulfed by failure and they are more likely to succeed next time round. Changing their beliefs about failure and success involves:

- seeing failure and poor performance as providing valuable feedback for improvement next time round
- recognizing that they can always improve
- realizing that there is usually a 'next time'
- recognizing that failure and poor performance say a lot about how hard they try, the way they do things and the knowledge they have – and that these can be improved
- setting realistic but challenging standards for their performance on upcoming tasks
- expanding their views of success to acknowledge and celebrate the many smaller gains they have made in their lives

These are just a few of the keys to eliminating the barriers to success. The chapters to follow identify many more opportunities to unlock students' academic potential.

11

DEVELOPING BROADLY BASED SELF-ESTEEM

If I don't do well I think, 'Oh no, I'm so dumb. I'm no good.

Cassie, age 17

The problem in a nutshell

Students who primarily base their self-esteem on their competence and how they perform are more likely to self-protect than students who are not so inclined to base their self-esteem on how they perform. As discussed in the beginning chapters, when students' self-esteem is overly dependent on successful performance, they place their self-esteem at risk. It is at risk because if they do not perform successfully, they can feel worthless. This places pressure on students every time they go into situations in which it is important to perform. This pressure can be intense because the stakes are so high – their very worth is up for grabs. This is why in situations in which students fear they might fail or perform poorly, many aim to protect their self-esteem.

Students who primarily base their self-esteem on how they perform usually make a fundamental mistake: they tend to equate cleverness and competence with high worth and equate incompetence with low worth. This is where much of their difficulties begin and this is why failure or poor performance are so feared – failure or poor performance reflect poorly on their competence or cleverness and this implies they are low in worth. Students are therefore primarily motivated to avoid failure or poor performance and earlier chapters outlined the variety of ways they do this through self-defeating protective behaviour. What students need to do, therefore, is to minimize the link between their competence and their self-esteem. When students see their competence and self-esteem as less connected, they are not so fearful of failure or poor performance because they do not ultimately reflect poorly on their worth.

What should students' self-esteem be based on?

Students' worth should not be solely dependent on their ability to perform on a test, succeed on the sporting field or top the class. As soon as they excessively tie their worth to these factors, they are vulnerable. If they do not perform well in the test then they feel they are worthless. The more students tie their worth to such outcomes, the more vulnerable they become. The more vulner-

123

able they become, the more they seek opportunities to avoid failure or poor performance and self-protect. Self-defeating protective behaviour is an attractive alternative for many students.

Teacher Tip 5

Encourage students to see that their fundamental worth as a person is not dependent on their ability to perform; rather, their performance reflects more on their effort, strategy, and attitude

---

This Teacher Tip looks simple enough, but in actual fact it requires a profound shift in how students think about themselves and what factors underpin their worth. It means flying in the face of institutional, family, social, and even personal pressures and assumptions. As children, we are quick to learn that students who are the brightest tend to be valued more highly than students who are not so academically bright. As teenagers, we learn that the best-looking guys and girls are afforded higher status than those who are not so good looking. On the sporting field we hold in high esteem those who shoot more goals, score more points, run or swim faster. As a society, we assign greater worth and esteem to those who are wealthier, more successful or famous than those who are not.

Here it is suggested that if students' worth is to be tied to anything, it should be tied to more helpful factors. One such factor is how hard they try. Another is whether they have done the best they can possibly do given the circumstances. These are not soft options, nor do they mean students resign themselves to mediocrity. If students perform the best that they can, what more can be asked of them? Importantly, basing their worth on performing the best that they can does not prevent the high achievers from achieving. On the contrary, it ensures they achieve while also ensuring the dignity and worth of those who do not perform at such high levels. In so doing, the majority of students are elevated from a self-esteem underclass to a sense of dignity and worth.

Teacher Tip 6

Show students that their effort, strategy, and attitude are much sounder bases for their self-esteem than their cleverness – importantly, effort, strategy and attitude can be improved at any time

---

Conclusion

When students no longer live in fear of failure and how it may damage self-esteem, they are in a stronger position to perform successfully. This is because they can dedicate more of their resources to performing on the task and not on self-protection through self-defeating behaviours. This view on self-esteem discourages passivity, complacency and mediocrity. Asking students to try as hard as they can and doing their best are rigorous standards and is asking no less than they are capable of delivering.

What are the consequences of this effort-based self-esteem? For a start, success and failure are within their control because they decide whether to try hard and do the best that they can. The fact that the outcome and their worth are more controllable takes some of the anxiety out of performance. With this anxiety gone, there is no longer the need to engage in failure-avoiding self-protection strategies; rather, students see their worth in terms of effort and trying hard and these are within students' reach.

12

EFFECTIVELY DEALING WITH COMPETITION

If I tell my family that I got 20 out of 20, that's the bit they care about. If I go home and say, 'Hey, I learnt that such and such is such and such,' they'd say, 'Oh that's great honey, but what did you get in your assignment?'

Brett, age 17

I feel most successful outperforming others. Don't get me wrong, I would rather feel better by mastering something, but it's all about competition. If you're doing better than others, then you know you're doing well, and that's how you gauge yourself.

Kate, age 17

The beliefs that accompany students' competitiveness

Before outlining the ways students' competitiveness gets them into difficulty, it is important to stress that competition has its place. It can motivate, energize and bring out students' best performance. Unfortunately, it also has the potential to paralyze students. Later in the book, it is described how a particular type of competition can be quite a positive force. For now, however, we look at the downside of competitiveness because it is another risk factor that can motivate self-defeating protective behaviour.

Competitive students feel successful when they outperform others, know more than others, get to the top, and demonstrate their competence for others to see. These students are concerned about how their competence and cleverness compare with others' cleverness and competence. Critically, it is their focus on their competence or cleverness (rather than their effort) that puts them at risk. They see success and failure in terms of their cleverness and comparative competence and not as a reflection of how much effort they have invested.

Thus, competitive students tend to see failure or poor performance due to incompetence. Because incompetence is so often linked with low worth and this evokes low self-esteem, competitive students can be particularly vulnerable in the face of possible failure or poor performance. This is a lethal combination – failure or poor performance due to incompetence linked to self-esteem.

The effects of competitive environments

Importantly, it is not just students' competitiveness that can be a problem. Oftentimes they must operate in quite competitive environments. Classrooms, for example, are particularly competitive. Research is emerging that shows that competitive environments can motivate some students to engage in self-defeating protective behaviour.

Certainly, competitive climates suit some students and bring out their best performance, as mentioned earlier in this chapter. We need only look at elite athletes who perform at their highest levels in competition. Having said this, however, how often have we seen these elite athletes 'choke' under pressure? It seems that even the elite can have difficulty in excessively competitive environments.

Are your students competitive?

To determine whether students are competitive, ask the following questions:

- Do students feel more successful outperforming others in a test or do they feel more successful learning the material for it?
- Do students feel better beating someone on an assignment or do they feel better having a challenge on the assignment that develops their skill?
- Do students feel more successful knowing more than others or do they feel more successful developing their knowledge?
- Do students feel more successful topping the class or do they feel more successful trying their hardest and doing their best?

If the answer is 'yes' to the first parts of the above questions, then your students are most likely competitive students. If the answer is 'yes' to the second parts of the questions, then your students are more mastery-oriented (see below). Some, however, may have identified with both parts of the questions. That's fine – this will be dealt with later as well.

What is the alternative to competitiveness?

What alternative is there to competitiveness? Well, there is a very feasible alternative in the form of mastery. Whereas competitive people feel successful demonstrating their cleverness or competence, mastery-oriented people feel successful learning, solving problems, gaining mastery, understanding new concepts and developing new skills. Most importantly, they do not see their success and failure so much in terms of competence. Rather, they see success and failure more in terms of how much effort they have invested. The competitive person sees failure or poor performance in terms of incompetence (which renders their self-esteem vulnerable). The mastery-oriented person, on the other hand, sees failure or poor performance in terms of insufficient effort. Unlike insufficient cleverness or competence, insufficient effort does not reflect poorly on students' worth and consequent self-esteem. Because of this, the mastery-oriented student does not fear failure or poor performance. In fact, mastery-oriented students see failure or poor performance as important diagnostic feedback that can be used to improve their next performance.

Coordinating competitiveness and mastery

As mentioned earlier, competitiveness need not be disadvantageous. Some students prefer at least some level of competition. Indeed, competitiveness has been found to lead to positive outcomes under particular conditions. It would therefore be misleading to dismiss competitiveness outright. Indeed, research has suggested that an element of competitiveness can energize and motivate the student.

What has recently been suggested is that some students can coordinate their competitiveness and mastery orientations. These students know when one is appropriate and the other is not. Academic life is complex and to adhere to one particular strategy all the time may not be the smartest way to operate. Students are constantly presented with a diversity of demands that in some cases require them to be competitive and in other cases require them to take the time to learn new material and master challenges. For example, during term students aim to master material and at exam time they become more competitive. Thus, they give themselves the best opportunities to learn and master important material and then are energized at the important times they need to perform in competitive situations.

This means that when students are in an exam situation, they might not ponder every aspect of their answer to ensure that it is perfect. In exam situations they might not have the time to master every aspect of the task. Rather, it is a race against the clock to communicate to the examiner as quickly and comprehensively as they can what they know about the area; that is, these students have to turn up their competitiveness and to some extent turn down the mastery. They learn to coordinate the two to best fit their circumstances and the demands before them.

Tabatha, age 15, when given an assignment to do, takes great time and care to read all the available literature, plan the essay, work on many drafts, and compile an excellent response to the assignment question. In effect, she is extremely mastery-oriented. Unfortunately, however, when she sits for an exam – where she does not have a few weeks to ponder a question, cannot write and rewrite drafts, and even does not have much time to plan her approach – she does not cope. She cannot perform under a competitive pressure situation. Invariably, Tabatha does not answer all the questions, which is simply throwing marks away. She has not learnt how to coordinate her mastery with her competitiveness. If she does, she will be a formidable force. Not only will she have mastered the material before the exam, but she will also be able to apply what she has gained through mastery in a competitive way under competitive conditions.

Increasing the emphasis on personal bests (PBs)

However, getting a delicate balance between competitiveness and mastery can be difficult. PBs may be a better way to balance a mastery orientation with competitiveness. A student gets a PB when their level of performance, skill or knowledge is higher than or is as good as their previous best level of performance, skill or knowledge.

Focusing on PBs is an effective strategy because although students focus on their own standards and performance, it evokes the sort of energy that friendly competition can provide. This is because students compete with themselves. So, it is a great way to get the most out of a mastery focus and yet capture the best of a performance or competition focus.

Students like the idea of PBs. They feel a bit like an academic athlete racing against themselves and this is exciting for them and energizes them. Instead of looking around at everyone else's marks and how they compare, they are focused on their own game and trying hard for personal reasons rather than competitive reasons.

In fact, even very competitive schools, which hold more traditional views of success along the lines of being the best and beating others, find the idea of PBs appealing. These schools accept a focus on PBs because they allow for a bit of competition in that students compete with their own previous performance but also allow for a personalized marker of success in that one's own standards are most important.

What athletes will say is that taking a broader view of success – such as focusing on PBs and improvement – does not in any way harm performance. Similarly, focusing on PBs in no way compromises students' performance because we are asking excellence of that student. Importantly, however, it is excellence in personal and achievable terms.

In the following pages are some tools for promoting PBs in the classroom. On the first page is a teacher's PB score sheet. Here, students can be assessed on various academic dimensions from a PB perspective. In the following two pages are student PB worksheets that students can use to help them set, work towards and attain PBs in their academic lives.

PERSONAL BEST (PB) SCORESHEET

Name_____ Year_____ Class_____ Date_____

This term's mark (circle one)

3 points Around or above previous best
2 points Slightly below previous best
1 point   Well below previous best but put in reasonable effort to get this mark
0 points Well below previous best and put in little or no effort to get this mark

This term's enthusiasm/engagement/attitude (circle one)

3 points Around or above previous best
2 points Slightly below previous best
1 point   Well below previous best but put in reasonable effort to get involved
0 points Well below previous best and put in little or no effort to get involved

Skills/competences developed this term (circle one)

3 points Around or above previous best
2 points Slightly below previous best
1 point   Well below previous best but put in reasonable effort to develop skills
0 points Well below previous best and put in little or no effort to develop skills

Golden point (circle if applicable to this student)

1 point   This term this student was committed to personal excellence

TOTAL PB SCORE / 10   **(Previous PB score** / 10)

0--3 points
Overall, well below PB
– Needs most work

4--6 points
Overall, below PB
– Needs some work

7--9 points
Overall, around or above PB
– Keep up the good work

10 points
Achieved personal excellence
– Keep up the excellent work

This student can get closer to his/her PB by:

1. _____

2. _____

This student can sustain his/her PB by:

1. _____

2. _____

PERSONAL BEST (PB) WORKSHEET

A PB is where you aim to match or better a previous best performance. It can be a mark you are aiming for or you can aim to do your schoolwork or study in a way that is an improvement on last time or the way you usually do it.

A. My PB is a mark in_____What mark are you aiming for?_____
OR
B. My PB is a better way of doing my schoolwork or study in_____

The better way of doing things is:_____

Is this PB maintaining a previous best or improving on a previous best?　YES/NO
If NO, you need to develop a PB that does.

Do you believe you can reach this PB?　　　　　　　　　　　　YES/NO
If NO, you need to develop a PB that you believe you can reach.

When do you plan to achieve this PB?_____

Describe the steps involved in reaching your PB	✓when achieved
1. First, I will	
2. Next, I will	
3.	
4.	
5.	
6.	
7.	
8.	
9.	
10.	

☐ I believe I reached my PB　　　　Evidence_____

☐ I think I just missed out　　　　Because _____

☐ I didn't get close to my PB　　　Because _____

My next PB is:_____

SAMPLE PERSONAL BEST (PB) WORKSHEET

A PB is where you aim to match or better a previous best performance. It can be a mark you are aiming for or you can aim to do your schoolwork or study in a way that is an improvement on last time or the way you usually do it.

A. My PB is a mark in_____ What mark are you aiming for?_____
OR
B. My PB is a better way of doing my schoolwork or study in *History*_____

The better way of doing things is: *I aim to be more organized when doing my next essay and plan things out a bit better before I start it*

Is this PB maintaining a previous best or improving on a previous best?   YES
If NO, you need to develop a PB that does.

Do you believe you can reach this PB?   YES
If NO, you need to develop a PB that you believe you can reach.

When do you plan to achieve this PB? *Next Friday 30th May (when it's due)*

Describe the steps involved in reaching your PB	✓ when achieved
First I will *understand the question*	✓
Next I will *break question into parts*	✓
Initial search for information (on the Internet and at the library)	✓
Focused and detailed reading of books and other resources collected	✓
Detailed summary of information	✓
Organize information (put information under each heading)	x
Write first draft of essay	✓
Tie up loose ends (e.g. do a bit more reading, ask teacher anything I don't know)	✓
Write second draft of essay	✓
Edit the essay (check spelling, grammar, formatting)	x
Write final draft and hand it in	✓

I believe I reached my PB   Evidence *I did most of the steps, more than I've done before*

☐ I think I just missed out   Because _____

☐ I didn't get close to my PB   Because _____

My next PB is: *I aim to get more than 70% on my next History essay*

Reducing comparisons with others

The more students have their attention focused on how they compare with others, the less attention they can give their schoolwork. Comparing themselves with others also takes the focus off their own standards and PBs and onto others' standards. Further, when students do not match up to others successfully, they can become deflated and lose their motivation to try next time.

It is therefore important to reduce the extent to which students are compared with other students and increase the extent to which they are their own benchmark. Certainly, it may be evident how students compare with each other, but avoid pointing this out to them. Instead, focus on the task, what can be learnt from the mark or feedback students received, how their mark or feedback compares with their previous performance, and the best ways to improve next time.

Another important strategy is to catch students putting themselves down compared to other students. This will not do much to help them next time they have to do an exam or assignment. This is a good opportunity to gently encourage students to see that they are their own benchmark and to show them that their focus should be on themselves and their potential, and not on how better or worse they do than other students.

Teacher Tip 7

In students' academic lives, there is both a need for mastery and a need for competitiveness. PBs are a great way to coordinate the two. Reducing comparisons with others is also important

---

Mastering competitiveness!

Importantly, students can take a mastery approach to learning how to be competitive! Yes, students can learn how to be competitive in effective ways.

Most students hate exams. One reason is because exams only happen a few times a year and so are relatively unfamiliar situations. Also, students rarely know what the specific exam questions will be. Essentially, much uncertainty surrounds exams and this usually arouses fear. In addition to this, the pressure cooker situation of limited time puts even more heat on students. Hence, the exam situation is an important competitive event that evokes anxiety and a fear of failure or poor performance and because of this, it is fertile ground for self-defeating protective behaviour.

But why should these situations be fraught with so much uncertainty, unfamiliarity and anxiety? They needn't be. For example, the final exams need not be a one-off pressure cooker event. Students can do sample exam questions under exam conditions at home. By the time these students get to the school hall for the finals, they are highly prepared and familiar with most of the questions and question types. In fact, by going over past exam questions, students often find that the differences in questions from year to year are not that great. Thus, in preparing thoroughly they find that there are recurring themes from test to test and the questions they answer in the finals are not much different from the ones they answered under exam conditions at home. Essentially, then, they adopt a mastery approach to prepare for a competitive situation. They accrue many hours practising their application of the mastered material under pressure conditions. By the time they get to the finals, they have mastered the material under pressure conditions and are not bluffed by the highly competitive situation.

Teacher Tip 8

Show students how their performance very much depends on their prior mastery and not so much on their competitiveness

---

What about performance anxiety? Students may have mastered the material, but when they open that exam paper, they crumble. It may appear that no amount of mastery can overcome this type of anxiety. For two reasons it is argued that this need not be the case. First, it is well established that through drill, deliberate practice, and over-learning, students can alleviate performance anxiety. Second, the reason why students experience performance anxiety is because they interpret competition as testing their cleverness or competence rather than testing their mastery. When students see competition along these lines, they will most certainly feel unpleasant in competitive situations because they see their performance as reflecting directly on their competence. On the other hand, seeing their capacity to perform in competitive situations as due to their prior mastery and preparation and not so much due to their competence ensures that students' self-esteem is intact if they do not do so well. This takes much of the anxiety out of the competitive situation.

It is important to emphasize here that if students are to be competitive – which in many settings they are – a failure to compete successfully should not be seen in terms of a lack of competence. Rather, they must see this so-called 'failure' as due to their preparation, the strategies they used, the knowledge and skills they acquired and address these. Essentially, then, when students do not compete successfully, they must look to how well they had mastered and prepared for the task and not look to their lack of competence.

Teacher Tip 9

Show students how thinking differently about competition (e.g. as reflecting on mastery and effort rather than competence) can help them deal more effectively with competitive environments and situations

---

Competition is a fundamental part of life – be it in education, business, social circles or sport. Because of this, it is important that students view competition as reflecting on their mastery and effort more than on their competence.

Competition at the classroom level

It is not uncommon for classrooms to be overly competitive, and this may evoke problematic behaviour. If the environment is overly competitive there is the very real possibility that success, failure and poor performance reflect more on students' competence than their effort. When students see their failure or poor performance in terms of incompetence – and hence self-esteem – then they will go to great lengths to protect themselves.

Thus, the notion that competition and ambition bring out the best in students may not always hold true. For some students, competition may bring out their best, but for many others, their best may be brought out under different conditions. This may mean promoting more of a mastery ethos in the classroom.

The reality is that there are deadlines and performance goals to reach. But there is no reason why these cannot be accommodated under mastery conditions. Competition and performance in the classroom can be recast to reflect students' effort rather than on their inherent ability. Thus, an inability to shape up to the classroom demands must be seen in terms of the amount and nature of effort students expend and not on their ability. For the most part, this would simply mean training, tutoring or mentoring so that more effective and efficient study and schoolwork practices are employed.

Teacher Tip 10

Through a focus on mastery, process outcomes, PBs and recognizing students' fundamental worth, educators can reshape learning environments to reduce negative effects of competition

---

Conclusion

This chapter has spent time on competition, how it can get students into difficulty, and how it can be recast to get students out of difficulty. The downside of competition is that success, failure and poor performance under competitive conditions tend to be seen in terms of students' competence and not in terms of their effort and mastery. As has been consistently argued, because students tend to equate low ability with low self-esteem, this means competition is potentially threatening to their self-esteem. Nevertheless, competition is here to stay, so students need to learn how to deal with it in a way that does not threaten their self-esteem and prompt them to sabotage their chances of success. To do this it is suggested that:

- students learn how to coordinate mastery and competitiveness
- students develop more of a PBs focus to their schoolwork
- students aim to reduce their comparisons with other students

- students see their performance in competition as reflecting on the extent to which they have mastered and tried, and not as reflecting on their intrinsic competence and worth as a person
- teachers recast competitive learning environments so that success, failure and poor performance are seen in terms of the amount of effort, skills, strategies and preparation applied and not in terms of high or low competence.

13

REDUCING
AVOIDANCE AND
INCREASING
SUCCESS
ORIENTATION

I study just to avoid failing. I just want to get through rather than try to do well.

Lachlan, age 17

What is avoidance orientation?

We have seen that students can be high or low in competitiveness and mastery orientation. There is another orientation. It relates to the student who tends to work hard not so much to beat others or master something, but to avoid failure or poor performance. These students can perform well, but they do so for unhelpful reasons. They are motivated to perform well not to succeed but to avoid failure or poor performance. As one student put it, 'I'm the one that's avoiding failure. I just don't want to fail in case my family says, "Oh, you're dumb, you can't do it"'. This is referred to as 'avoidance orientation' and has recently received more detailed attention in the research community.

Students become avoidance-oriented because they hold doubts about their competence and cleverness and tend to dwell on the possibility of failure or poor performance more than others. Failure and poor performance become the reference points and the impetus to perform. Because these people tend to dwell on failure or poor performance, they are also more likely to be motivated to self-protect.

Take the case of Meredith, age 15, who plays basketball for the school. She is not the best player in the team, but certainly is not the worst. The team is doing well in the competition and as the end of the season draws near, winning every game becomes critical to them qualifying for the finals. Meredith feels this pressure acutely and becomes increasingly doubtful about her competence as a player and lives in constant fear that she will let the team down. Whereas early in the season when there was not so much pressure to do well, she enjoyed the exercise, developing her basketball skills and scoring some baskets, her main goal now is to avoid letting the team down. Essentially, she has become avoidance-oriented: motivated to avoid failure or poor performance and their negative consequences.

As the end of the season approaches and failure and poor performance loom larger than ever, she begins to dedicate her

---

energies to self-protection more than improving her basketball. She starts missing practice sessions on the pretext that she has to work back late in class. Soon she is dropped back to the reserve bench – a position she feels much more comfortable with and eventually is not even called onto the court. Thus, her avoidance orientation has prompted her to manoeuvre defensively and this eventually leads to honourable discharge. Honourable because she has managed to fail with dignity. But it is clearly counter-productive because through her defensive manoeuvring Meredith has cut herself off from the possibility of success and the joys of participation and team membership. Possibly worst of all, she has set a precedent of self-protective withdrawal that she will find more difficult to resist next time she doubts herself. The ultimate tragedy is that she will increasingly cut herself off from new and challenging experiences that would ultimately extend and better her.

It is evident, then, that an avoidance orientation is a risk factor that can contribute to counterproductive behaviour. To what extent are your students avoidance-oriented and motivated more to avoid failure than to succeed or master? Ask the following questions:

- When students are engaged in a challenging task, do they find themselves preoccupied with the possibility of failure or poor performance?
- Do students work hard to avoid failure or poor performance rather than strive for success?
- Does avoiding failure or poor performance become the main reasons students work hard at a task?
- Is avoiding negative reactions from others the main reason students work hard at a task?

If the answer is 'yes' to these questions, then students are to some degree avoidance-oriented and this can manifest itself in any number of problematic academic behaviours.

Why do students become avoidance-oriented?

Ideally, students should be more motivated to perform out of a desire to achieve success than to avoid failure or poor performance. Unfortunately, however, this orientation is not always easy to maintain. To become success-focused, students need to address the very reasons why they became avoidance-oriented in the first place.

The major reason – and the one this book keeps returning to – is that students see their cleverness as tied to their worth as a person and this is linked to their self-esteem. When students' self-esteem is dependent on their competence or cleverness, suddenly every performance and evaluation is something to be feared. They are feared because at every step, students' self-esteem is at risk. When this is the case, it is really not so surprising that they decide to play it safe and protect what gains they may have made up to that point. Thus, students become avoidance-oriented – motivated to avoid looking dumb or incompetent. When students are motivated to avoid looking dumb or incompetent, they cannot be success-focused.

Another reason students become avoidance-oriented is because they see failure or poor performance as evidence of a lack of competence or cleverness and hence a lack of worth, and not as the bases for improvement in the future. When they see failure as defining their worth as a person, students' priority is to avoid it. When students' priority is to avoid failure or poor performance, they cannot be success-focused.

A further reason students become failure-avoidant is because the environment in which they operate makes avoiding failure the focus. These environments do not motivate students to succeed out of a desire for success; rather, these environments attempt to motivate success through a fear of failure or poor performance. This may work for a while. But after some time, this failure avoidance becomes the priority and even becomes more important than success itself.

Teacher Tip 11

Teach students how to recognize environments and situations that might trigger a fear of failure and encourage them to focus more on the work to be accomplished and mastery of that work – and less on how their work will be evaluated or compared to someone else

---

An environment in which failure or poor performance do not reflect poorly on students' worth, an environment where the aim is to bring out the best in students, an environment that respects personal goals and standards set by the student, and an environment that is not a zero-sum game in terms of reward (e.g. one student getting the rewards or accolades at the expense of the other students) is an environment conducive to bringing out the best in students.

This discussion can be extended to the family. It is perhaps not surprising that families can foster a failure-avoidance climate. For example, on zero-sum reward games, it is often the case in families that children are rewarded at the expense of their siblings. This sets up a competitive climate and as was seen earlier, a competitive climate is one where competence and cleverness, how one is evaluated, and how one compares to others are the foci. When these are the foci, failure or poor performance tend to reflect poorly on a child's worth and once this happens, families become fertile ground for failure avoidance. It must be recognized that children have different abilities and skills and that standards for one child are not necessarily applicable to another. Following from this, it is important to encourage children to aspire to standards that are meaningful and realistic for them and also which are developed from their perspective and not from the perspective of external standards about what should and should not be the case.

Again, the idea of personal bests (PBs) rather than outperforming others is one to consider. It goes without saying that PBs and outperforming others are not mutually exclusive. One can achieve a PB and outperform others. The difference is that the PB is the focus and performance under these conditions is one in which the individual is success-focused and not failure-avoidant. Also, zero-sum reward games (where one child gets a reward and another misses out) only breed competition between siblings and while they communicate success to one child, they communicate failure to the other. Unfortunately, children often equate failure with a lack of worth and so they become motivated to avoid failure through any number of self-defeating behaviours.

Teacher Tip 12

Encourage students to understand that focusing on mastery and improvement promotes a success focus and minimizes fear of failure and self-defeating behaviour

---

Conclusion

An avoidance orientation is one in which the student is motivated primarily to avoid failure or poor performance rather than strive for success. Not only does this evoke a negative focus (on failure or poor performance), but it makes the student vulnerable to problematic behaviour. Major causes of an avoidance orientation include linking competence to self-esteem, linking failure or poor performance to incompetence rather than effort, and avoidance-oriented environments. When students change the way they view failure or poor performance, the bases of their self-esteem, and the environments in which they operate, they become success-focused and in doing so increase their chances of success.

14

DEVELOPING HEALTHY VIEWS OF COMPETENCE

Two ways to view competence

How students see their competence can also motivate them to engage in problematic behaviour. Essentially, students can see their competence as fixed, which cannot be changed; or, they can see their competence as something that can be developed and improved on. Importantly, when students see their competence as fixed and which cannot be changed they are more likely to be motivated to self-protect.

Consider a situation in which Rosemary, age 20, a trainee teacher, bombed her first lesson to a class because she lost control of the students' behaviour. If she saw her ability to exercise effective discipline as something that was fixed and which could not be changed, then she would think that there was nothing she could do to improve on her previous lesson. This is fertile terrain for self-protective behaviour. Sadly, this is exactly what Rosemary thought about her ability to control her class. She believed that there was nothing she could do to improve her performance in the classroom and at the time I spoke to her, she was neglecting her studies and was seriously considering dropping out of her course. She would rather withdraw with what dignity she had left than risk failure again.

Take the example of Peter, age 17, who considers himself to be a poor dancer. He sees his competence as a dancer as something that is fixed and which cannot be improved. As far as he is concerned, he is stuck with others seeing him as an incompetent dancer. He deals with this by drinking before he goes to the school dance (a self-handicapping strategy). This way, he is loosened up a little and his poor performance can be at least partly attributed to the alcohol. In fact, if for some reason there is no opportunity for him to drink, he would rather not go to the school dance at all.

James, age 17, is also a rather clumsy dancer. However, he sees his dancing competence as something that can be developed and improved on. In holding this view of his dancing competence, he is much more optimistic about his ability to improve. Also, because of this optimism, he takes active steps to improve his dancing by asking his older sister to teach him some dance moves. In contrast to Peter, who seems to contribute further to his clumsiness by drinking alcohol or avoiding school dances, James aims to maximize his chances of future success. There is no need for James to self-protect because he is optimistic and quite clearly sees ways in which he can improve his dancing. Essentially, Peter and James can be separated on the basis of their views about their competence. One holds a fixed view, while the other sees that his competence can be developed and improved upon.

How students' views of their competence influence their goals

It has also been found that students who hold a fixed view of their competence have different goals and priorities than those who hold the view that their competence can be developed and improved. Students who see their competence as something that can be improved tend to pursue goals aimed at attaining mastery, solving problems, learning new things and improving themselves. In fact, rather than flee from difficult and challenging tasks, these students actually embrace these challenges because it is through these tasks that they are able to develop their competence. Thus, far from attempting to avoid failure or self-protect in anticipation of failure or poor performance, these students see their mistakes as valuable feedback for how they can improve next time round.

Students who see their competence as something that is fixed and cannot be improved have different goals. They are more interested in avoiding negative judgements about their competence. Again, this links back to the idea that they see competence as something they are stuck with. Because they feel they are stuck with low competence, they also fear that they are stuck with others' poor opinion of their competence and so their priority becomes one of avoiding others' poor opinion of them. Essentially, then, students who hold a fixed view of intelligence and competence are more interested in concealing incompetence from others.

Take the example of Stephen, age 16, who is in senior high school. He sees his competence in maths as fixed and believes that no amount of effort can significantly improve his skill in this area. Rather than turn his efforts to developing his maths competence, he turns his efforts to manoeuvring so that he can conceal his incompetence. He tends to leave his homework and study to the last minute, conveniently leaves his textbook at school the night before the exam, misbehaves during class, and never really puts any effort into maths problems he is assigned. Through these self-handicapping behaviours, he manages to muddy the waters. No one can really conclude that he is incompetent because he ensures there is never really a fair test of his competence. He has therefore concealed his possible incompetence from others, but as has been pointed out earlier, this only works for a while. Stephen may eventually get trapped in a downward performance pattern and people may begin to suspect his competence – something he has been at pains to avoid. By this time he has put himself into an unwinnable position from which it is difficult to recover.

Students' views of their competence and how they see failure or poor performance

Students who see their competence as something they can improve on are not threatened by failure or poor performance. Instead, they see failure or poor performance as something they can use to improve later performance.

Take the case of Catherine, age 17, who is in Stephen's maths class. She believes that her competence in maths is not fixed but something that she can develop given sufficient effort. She is not motivated to conceal her possible incompetence (as Stephen is). Rather, she is motivated to work hard, learn from her mistakes, and do all that it takes to achieve her personal best (PB). In fact, whereas Stephen tackles tasks that are far too easy or far too difficult for him (i.e. tasks that guarantee success or that cannot be a fair test of his competence or cleverness), Catherine tackles tasks that are realistic challenges that extend her.

149

It is clear, then, that holding a fixed view of competence or cleverness renders students vulnerable when they fail. It makes them feel worthless, they do not recover from the failure or poor performance very easily, and they are fearful that they will fail again. The ground is then fertile for self-protective action. As above, Peter, who believes his competence as a dancer cannot be improved, drinks or avoids to self-protect and Stephen, who sees his competence in maths as fixed, procrastinates and does not try.

Changing the way students view their competence

The issue, then, is how students see their competence or cleverness. Probably they will have a different view of their competence in different areas of their lives. Students may feel they can improve on their tennis game with sufficient effort but not improve their ability to write essays, or vice versa. Also, the areas of their lives that need closer consideration are those that are important to how they feel about themselves and their self-esteem. For example, tennis may be just a fun activity to let off steam at the end of the week and to mix with friends. Being good or bad at it does not really have much bearing on a student's self-esteem. So, having a fixed view of competence in this area probably does not matter much.

On the other hand, students' performance in school may be important to their feelings about themselves. When their teacher tells them their essays need a lot of work, they feel pretty lousy. In terms of their self-esteem, this is a quite different situation from the tennis game and so needs attention. If students see their essay writing as something that is fixed and which cannot be improved, then they will feel pessimistic. If they see their essay writing as something that can improve, then they will be more optimistic about their ability to improve and tend to see the teacher's feedback as constructive rather than damaging.

When students believe there is hope for improvement, they are likely to tackle the task in a constructive and proactive way. When students see that they are stuck with their essay writing skill, they do not see hope for improvement, and they are likely to dedicate more effort to manoeuvring in a self-protective way than apply effort to improve. This manoeuvring might take the form of not caring about how they write and not investing sufficient effort (in which case they can only be accused of not trying or caring and not of being a poor essay writer) or it may be as drastic as dropping the subject altogether (in which case their competence is not tested at all).

To address faulty beliefs about the nature of competence and cleverness, it is important to focus on competence as something that can be developed. Before doing this, however, students must first be convinced that this is true. This raises the question: Are students stuck with their competence or can they develop and improve on it?

Researchers have shown that the vast majority of many tasks assigned to students can be mastered through hard work, careful problem solving and study skills, practice, planning, organization and help-seeking. Thus, students can develop many of the skills that are needed to succeed to their potential at school.

It is important to reiterate the idea of the 'success zone' here. For any given skill and competence at school each student has a success zone. While their genetics, their upbringing and their environment are significant contributors to their success zones, it is also what students do and think today that determines where they are located in these zones.

The other point important to emphasize is that for most students, their success zones are wide, not narrow. This is very important to recognize. A wide success zone means that a student who experiences failure is not restricted to this outcome. With the appropriate assistance and motivation, that student's success zone probably extends to 'pass' territory and with further application, performance well beyond this.

If we consider students' competence and skills in terms of success zones that can be improved, then it necessarily follows that their competence and skills can be developed. When viewed in this light, students have reason for optimism. Perhaps more importantly, when viewed in these terms, students have little reason to self-protect because the failure or poor performance that they fear can be overcome through the development of competence and skill.

Teacher Tip 13

Show students that for any given competence or skill, they have room to move – upwards and downwards – and they have much control over this

---

Effort (how hard students work), strategy (how they do that work) and attitude (what they think about themselves, school, schoolwork and teachers) are crucial ingredients in whether students move beyond where they are at present. It does not happen just because they want it to happen. There is no getting around the fact that to develop their potential students must work at it. They must take the time to learn the skills required to work more efficiently, to manage their time better, and to organize and present their material more effectively. These are skills developed through hard work and dedication.

Teacher Tip 14

Teach students that competence and skills are developed through effort (how hard they work), strategy (how they do that work) and attitude (what they think about themselves, school, schoolwork and teachers)

Conclusion

When students see their competence, cleverness and skills as things they can improve on and develop, they will see a number of other things differently as well. They will find that through healthy views of competence:

- rather than avoid difficult or challenging tasks, they will embrace these tasks because they are an excellent way to develop skills
- they will become more interested in the task and less interested in how they are being evaluated by others
- they will be less interested in trying to conceal possible incompetence from others
- they will see success, failure and poor performance as due to effort and not due to possible incompetence
- they will become optimistic and success-focused rather than pessimistic and failure avoidant.

15

DEVELOPING ROCK-SOLID SELF-ESTEEM

What is a shaky self-esteem and why is it a problem?

Students' feelings about themselves can change a great deal. For example, they may feel good about themselves one day or in one situation and not so good about themselves the next. Their feelings about themselves can even vary from hour to hour. When students' feelings about themselves fluctuate a good deal, they are said to have a shaky, unstable or uncertain self-esteem.

Students who are shaky in their self-esteem are prime candidates at risk of problematic academic orientations. Because their self-esteem is shaky, they are uncertain about how they can tackle upcoming tasks. They may therefore contemplate and fear the possibility of failure or poor performance. As consistently shown throughout this book, when students fear failure or poor performance, they run the risk of self-defeating protective behaviour.

Richard, age 17, has a shaky belief in his ability to socialize at a youth group meeting. Usually he can hold his own when required, but he is constantly unsure about whether he is particularly interesting to talk to and is always frightened that he will run out of things to talk about, ask dumb questions or make inane observations. Before a youth group meeting, he will try to build up his confidence, telling himself that he is an interesting person to talk to, but as soon as someone seems to display a lack of interest in him or his conversation, he is crushed and thinks he is hopeless. Essentially, then, Richard's social self-esteem is very shaky.

Richard has developed a few strategies to deal with his shaky belief in himself. He chooses really easy or really difficult people or groups to engage. He may zero in on the person who is also clearly having difficulty at the youth group – the loner. This person is unlikely to reject him because they too are in need of company. On other occasions he targets the most popular group or the most beautiful girl. If they reject him, he can breathe easy in the sense that it was not a fair test of his social competence and therefore cannot be taken as proof of incompetence. At other times, he has been known to withdraw from the youth group and leave early. In all cases, Richard's behaviour is motivated out of a fear of failure or poor performance and the need to protect his shaky self-esteem.

How shaky is your students' self-esteem?

- Do your students experience marked fluctuations in how they feel about themselves?
- Do your students change from a very good opinion of themselves to a very poor one?
- Do your students' descriptions of themselves change from one day to the next?
- Do your students' beliefs about themselves conflict with how others see them?
- Do your students spend much time wondering about the kind of person they really are?
- Do your students think they know others better than they know themselves?

Answering 'yes' to these questions implies that your students have a shaky belief in themselves.

Why do students have a shaky self-esteem and how do we address it?

Why does Richard have a shaky belief in himself? Research has shown that students with a shaky self-esteem tend to overrely on others' evaluations of them. These students tend to place a great emphasis on how they are seen by others and this contributes to their shaky belief in a number of ways. First, these students can never truly know how others view them and so they find themselves changing their view of themselves depending on who they are interacting with. Second, the different people in students' lives all have differing views of them and so if these students rely on others' views of them to inform their own self-esteem, then it is no surprise that it is shaky. Another reason students can have a shaky self-esteem is because they base their self-esteem on their competence and demonstrations of their competence. Because students cannot be competent all the time, those who do base their self-esteem on competence will have a shaky self-esteem.

In developing strategies to deal with students' shaky self-esteem, it is important to recognize the causes of that shaky self-esteem. As mentioned above, one reason for shaky self-esteem is that students are dependent on how others respond to them. Because others' evaluations and opinions of students are unlikely to be consistent, their self-esteem is likely to be shaky. It is therefore essential that students separate their views and feelings about themselves from how they think others view them.

It is also risky for students to base their self-esteem on how others respond to them because they so often misinterpret others' behaviour. Students can recall dealings with teachers where they have got the distinct impression that the teacher is not happy with what the student has done or said. Students have made the mistake of carrying this away and being down on themselves only to find out later that the teacher was not feeling well or was not happy for some other reason. Basically, the students just happened to be in the wrong place at the wrong time. They had misinterpreted the situation.

Another reason students' self-esteem becomes shaky is because they base their feelings about themselves on others' assessments of them. Unfortunately, these assessments are often not consistent. For example, it has been found that teachers can provide inconsistent assessment and feedback. Teachers have also been found to reward students inconsistently. If students' self-esteem is based on these types of feedback, then it will be shaky. It is therefore important that if students use others' feedback to them as the basis for how they feel about themselves, then they need to recognize that the feedback may be inconsistent or even inappropriate.

Finally, when addressing students' shaky self-esteem, it is important to recognize that students often base their feelings about themselves on their demonstration of competence. Unfortunately, students cannot always be competent and so if they tie their self-esteem to their competence too closely, then it will be shaky. While it is difficult to separate self-esteem from competence, if students want to maintain a more stable self-esteem, it is important to do just this. Judgements of competence will vary based on the nature of the task, the evaluator and the conditions. If the task is something poorly designed or not fairly assessed and students base their self-esteem on performance on it, then their self-esteem will probably suffer. Because students cannot control the nature of the tasks presented to them or who will be assessing their performance, they put the stability of their self-esteem at risk if they base it on performance under such conditions.

Teacher Tip 15

Encourage students to minimize the extent to which their feelings about themselves are based on others' responses to them, others' evaluations of them, or their ability to be competent all the time

---

Conclusion

Students' shaky belief in themselves can render them vulnerable in the face of failure or poor performance. This is because they are uncertain about their ability to overcome this failure or poor performance. When students are uncertain in their ability to overcome failure or poor performance, they may choose to self-protect rather than strive for success. There are a number of ways to develop a more stable self-esteem. These include minimizing the extent to which students' feelings about themselves are based on others' responses to them or evaluations of them and their ability to be competent all of the time.

16
RUNNING YOUR OWN RACE

I'm not one to seek help from a teacher because I feel if you seek help, the teacher will think you're a dumb-ass and I don't want that to happen. Maybe I am a dumb-ass, but I just don't want other people to know.

Cooper, age 14

Public self-consciousness

As outlined earlier, a major part of students' fear of failure or poor performance is their fear that others will see them fail or perform poorly. The reason students so dislike others seeing them fail is because they often base their self-esteem on how others view their performance. If others see them fail, then it reflects poorly on their worth that in turn negatively affects their self-esteem. It is clear, then, that an over-concern with how others view them makes students' self-esteem vulnerable.

This tendency to be concerned with how one is viewed by others is called public self-consciousness. Students who are publicly self-conscious are concerned with how they appear to others and how others evaluate them. They are particularly fearful that others will disapprove of them and are motivated to avoid making a bad impression. Essentially, publicly self-conscious students are primarily interested in avoiding negative evaluations by others.

Very early on in their lives, these students learnt how it feels to perform poorly in class and for others to know about it. For example, they learnt how it feels to not know the answer to a question. In some ways, the public shame in knowing that everyone has seen them fail is worse than the private shame they feel. These students also learnt that in some cases it is better for their self-esteem to dedicate their energies to failing with dignity than dedicate their energies to try to succeed.

Not only can an over-concern with how others see them motivate these students to engage in self-defeating behaviour, but it can also create other pressures. These students can make others' standards of them more important than their own standards. These students become more anxious. They change the focus of the activity from one that they can learn from and enjoy to one dominated by the need to succeed in the eyes of others.

There are a variety of not so positive ways in which students respond to their concern about how others view them. We are well familiar with the students who 'choke' at a critical time in the school year. We are well familiar with students who refuse to participate in any school sport because of their fear of how they will be seen by others. We are well familiar with students who are too frightened to ask a question in class for fear they will be seen to be dumb. We know how terrifying it is for many students when exam results are posted on the notice board. We know about the many opportunities students miss because they do not want to risk being seen as having failed at them.

Do your students care how others view or evaluate them?

Essentially, then, students' public self-consciousness holds them back and the prime reason for this is because they do not want to be seen as incompetent and hence low in worth. Ask the following questions:

- Do your students care how others see them and their ability to perform?
- Do others' opinions impact on how your students see themselves?
- Do your students need the approval of others to feel good about themselves?
- Is it important to your students to avoid others' disapproval?

If the answer to these questions is 'yes', then your students' self-esteem is vulnerable to how others view them. As has been stated on a number of occasions, the ground is now fertile for self-defeating behaviour.

Some faulty assumptions

It would be simplistic and perhaps flippant to recommend that students not care what others think of them. We need to be a little more specific and get at the mechanics of students' concern about how others view them rather than simply telling them not to care how others view them.

Strategy requires that we address a number of assumptions that students make about their self-esteem and what determines it. Specifically, there are a number of faulty assumptions that need to be carefully scrutinized if students are to shift the basis of their worth away from how others view them. Some of these assumptions are as follows:

- 'I need your approval to feel good about myself'.
- 'Your opinion of me is more important than my opinion of myself'.
- 'What you think of me is extremely important to my life'.
- 'The more people approve or agree with me, the more worthwhile I am'.
- 'It is important that others evaluate me and my performance highly'.
- 'Other people's standards are more important than my own'.

These are core beliefs that can get students into difficulty. When students hold these beliefs, they make themselves vulnerable because they cannot control how others view or evaluate them. For example, if students are singularly motivated to avoid looking bad and they are presented with a difficult task that threatens failure or poor performance, they may find themselves strategically manoeuvring to protect their self-esteem. In this book, we have seen many examples where students engage in self-defeating protective behaviour when there is the chance that they may fail in the eyes of others.

Core beliefs are difficult to shake. Students must be highly attentive to them, quick to challenge them and challenge them consistently. Some challenging thoughts include:

- 'Your approval is nice to have but I don't need it to feel good about myself'.
- 'It is nice that your opinion of me is positive but my opinion of myself is more important'.
- 'What you think of me is really your business and not mine'.
- 'It is nice to have others approve or agree with me but it does not determine how worthwhile I am'.
- 'It is nice for others to evaluate me positively, but it is unlikely that they always will, and I am not less of a person if they don't'.
- 'Others' approval of me does not make me inherently more worthwhile'.
- 'My own standards are more important than the standards of others'.

What will be noticed here is that students do not deny the relevance of others in their lives. It is unrealistic for students to be totally unresponsive to others' opinions of them. Of course, students feel good when others approve of them or agree with what they have done, said or achieved. It is important not to deny the affirming role that others can play in their lives.

However, while it is nice to have others approve of them, students must be careful to separate this from their core beliefs about their value and worth. Students are simply not being fair to themselves when they make their fundamental worth dependent on others seeing them win the sporting event, excel in the exam, or be the life of the party. Conversely, students are not being fair to themselves if they devalue their worth when they lose the sporting event, perform poorly in the exam, or appear nervous and shy at the party.

Teacher Tip 16

Make it clear to students that while it is nice to have others' approval (or avoid their disapproval), it is not a measure of their worth

---

The pitfalls of public self-consciousness

What must also be understood is that when students care about how others view them, their self-esteem will be shaky. Up one day, down the next. After a while, this gets debilitating as they continually ride the roller coaster of approval and disapproval. The fact is that students simply cannot be approved of by everyone all the time, but many students assume uniform and continual approval is possible. It is students' faulty assumptions that undo them.

Another danger of trying to meet others' standards is that when these people are not present to observe or know about the performance, students are not motivated to perform. On the other hand, students who have been guided by their own standards and incentives are always motivated because their intrinsic motivation is ever present. Thus, if students place emphasis on what others think of them and are motivated by the need to gain or avoid their approval or disapproval, then when there is no audience they will not be motivated to perform because the external incentive is not present. When students only study to please the teacher or their parents, for example, if these people are not present or are unaware of whether the students are studying, they are less inclined to study. Conversely, when students study with the main purpose to improve skills and knowledge, it does not matter that there is no audience.

Giving priority to personal standards

The solution to students' over-concern with others' view of them is not so much to become less dependent on their approval and disapproval; rather, students need to develop and foster standards and values that are personally important to them.

One way to go about this would be to build on some of the principles established in this book. These include aspiring to master material or tasks rather than being concerned about beating or outperforming others; identifying the personal rewards that can be gained from a task rather than what external rewards can be gained; and, seeing performance in terms of personal bests (PBs) rather than in terms of comparisons with others. Each of these strategies shifts the focus away from others and onto the task and what students are capable of.

Teacher Tip 17

Encourage students to develop more personal and intrinsic reasons for doing their schoolwork. These reasons can involve satisfaction through mastery, desire for problem solving, development of new skills, striving for personal excellence, or the search for new understanding

---

Conclusion

Students can get themselves into difficulty when they base their self-esteem on others' approval and disapproval. First, it lays the foundation for self-defeating behaviour: they go to quite problematic lengths to protect their image in the eyes of others. Second, it puts students on an emotional roller coaster, ducking and weaving to please the variety of people in their lives. Third, it leaves them with a shaky self-esteem, built on others' approval. Finally, it can leave students unmotivated when others are not there to approve or disapprove of what they do.

Students can overcome these pitfalls by recognizing that their self-esteem is not dependent on whether others approve or disapprove of them. By supplementing this recognition with a set of personally developed standards and expectations (i.e. developed independently of others' standards and expectations), then students' self-esteem is not vulnerable in the event of failure or poor performance and they are not motivated to protect it through self-defeating behaviour.

17
SEIZING CONTROL

Even if I think I'll do very well, it turns out the opposite. You know, I think I'll get a really good mark and it ends up a Fail. That's why I've given up thinking I'll pass.

Charlotte, age 17

Students' uncertainty and how it develops

Students often engage in self-defeating protective behaviour because they are unsure about their ability to avoid failure or poor performance in upcoming tasks; that is, they are uncertain about how much control they have over whether they succeed or fail. As has been consistently argued, when students are faced with the possibility of failure or poor performance, their self-esteem is under threat; therefore, doubts about their ability to avoid failure or poor performance can give rise to self-protective behaviour that in many cases is quite problematic.

A major reason why students are uncertain about their control over avoiding failure or repeating success is because they are not sure of the reasons why they have failed or succeeded in the past. If students are unsure why they have failed in the past, then they will be unsure about how to avoid it in the future. If students are unsure about why they succeeded in the past, then they will be unsure about how to repeat that success in the future. If, on the other hand, students know why they failed, then they are usually in a better position to know how to avoid it in the future. Similarly, if students know what they did to bring about their previous success, then they usually know how to do it again. Essentially, then, when students know why they failed or succeeded, they feel more control over future outcomes and when students do not know why they failed or succeeded, they are uncertain about their ability to avoid failure or repeat success.

Students' experience of uncertain control

Unfortunately, most students have experienced 'non-contingent' outcomes in their academic life; that is, success or failure they do not really know the cause of. How often have students got a good exam mark and did not know how or why they performed well? It is possible it made them feel uncertain in their ability to repeat that success. What about an exam they did poorly in or failed and had no idea why? It is possible that on the next exam they were unsure about how to avoid failing again.

In both cases there is the potential to protect self-esteem in the next exam. In the situation where students do not know the cause of their success, they might decide that they do not want to jeopardize that success in the next exam and manoeuvre in a way that keeps their positive cleverness image intact. For example, the student who does well on a previous exam and does not know why might decide to do less study for the next exam. Certainly, he does not do nearly as well, but he can claim that he did not try so hard this time and point to his previous success as being the true indicator of his cleverness – he has protected his prior gain.

What about the student who failed an exam and did not know why? She does not want to risk further failure or poor performance, so she decides not to study. When she fails again, she cannot be accused of being incompetent; rather, she just did not try hard enough. Thus, while both students received quite different grades on a previous exam – one succeeded and one failed – both are motivated to self-protect because of their uncertain control in the next exam.

Indeed, we might need to rethink some of our approaches to how we reward students. We hear some teachers say that they try to reward their students at every opportunity so that the students develop a positive self-esteem. Unwittingly, however, this may contribute to students' uncertainty in future tasks. As discussed above, when students do not really know why they are being rewarded, they are not sure what they need to do in the future to be rewarded again. They may choose to play it safe and protect the gains they have made by engaging in self-defeating behaviour that enables them to fail with dignity and with their self-esteem intact.

'Non-contingent' outcomes are not limited to the school context. How many parents have set quite rigorous standards for the older child to achieve before she is rewarded but rewarded the younger child simply as a matter of course – just to be fair? It may be that they unwittingly create an uncertainty in the younger child as to what it takes to succeed or avoid failure or poor performance. What about when students are selected in a sporting team and they cannot understand why? Chances are they experience doubt as to how they can live up to that selection.

All these cases are examples of 'non-contingent' outcomes and the net result is uncertain control over one's ability to avoid failure or bring about success. This uncertainty influences the way students behave. When they are uncertain about future outcomes, they tend to behave in quite self-defeating ways that often ensure failure or poor performance – but failure with dignity that does not reflect poorly on their competence, cleverness and self-esteem.

What can be done to address students' uncertain control?

If a major source of students' uncertainty is how others reward or fail them, then it may be tempting to think that there is little they can do to avoid this. Not so. The most important thing students can do is to make the effort to find out exactly why they were rewarded or failed. Students need to empower themselves by establishing quite clearly the reasons for success, failure or poor performance. Thus, rather than assume they have little or no control over avoiding failure in the future, students need to be proactive and investigate the reasons for that failure. More than likely, they will find that there are some identifiable reasons why they failed or performed poorly that can be addressed next time. Whereas in the past they may have reacted to their uncertainty with some protective self-defeating behaviour, this time students have found out exactly why they have failed and are now armed with information to use to improve on their performance.

It is not easy to go back to the teacher who marked them poorly to ask the exact reasons for it. Usually, when students fail, they want to put it behind them and not have to face up to what they think it says about their competence and worth. But it is essential that students connect what they did with the outcome, because if they cannot connect them in any meaningful way, then they feel little or no control over avoiding it happening again.

All this takes courage. As one student who had experienced previous failure recognized, 'I've got to get up the guts to say to my teacher, "Hey, I screwed up. What can I do?"' What also helps is to fully understand that poor performance does not reflect on one's worth as a person; rather, it largely reflects on some of the strategies students used, their preparation, and the amount and nature of their effort.

In some ways it is a little trickier to find out why we succeeded when we are not sure of the reasons. Students do not want to jeopardize the mark they got by going back to the teacher to ask why they did well. Also, students do not want to jeopardize the positive image that they have gained. We might encourage students to ask how they might improve next time and what particular aspects of their schoolwork the teacher liked and did not like so much. Asking these types of probing questions will no doubt uncover much about the reasons why they did well. Armed with this information, students will feel more control over repeating that success next time.

Teacher Tip 18

When students succeed, fail or perform poorly and they do not know why, encourage them to find out why, with particular focus on what is in their control. This enhances their optimism for repeating that success or avoiding that failure or poor performance next time

---

Rewarding students

There is also a lesson here for reward systems. If students feel less control when they are rewarded or failed for no apparent reason, then teachers must question whether they should be rewarding and failing students in this way. A common mistake is to administer reward to students to make them feel good when they have not done anything that they can link to that reward. Certainly, teachers may have bolstered their self-esteem for a moment, but soon students start wondering how they are going to repeat this success because they do not know what caused it. This creates anxiety, a fear that they cannot repeat their success, and in many cases some manoeuvring designed to protect the gains they have made.

The onus, therefore, is on teachers to administer success and failure feedback that is directly and obviously connected to something students have done. Students must be in no doubt about why they are being rewarded or failed. And most importantly, students must be clear about how they can repeat that success or avoid that failure or poor performance in the future.

Teachers bring out the best in students when students have a sense of personal control over their ability to avoid failure or poor performance and maintain success. When students do not have this sense they are plagued with doubt, insecurity and fear. Following closely is self-defeating protective behaviour in the face of such uncertainty and insecurity. Among the most extreme forms of this self-defeating protective behaviour is learned helplessness and disengagement. Here the student is so convinced that there is nothing they can do to avoid failure or poor performance that they accept failure and give up trying.

Teacher Tip 19

When students receive feedback on their schoolwork, it is essential that they link this feedback to their behaviour (i.e. link their result to how hard they tried, the way they presented their work etc.). This feedback must also be followed up with clear information about what they can do to improve their performance or repeat their success

---

Conclusion

When students do not know the reasons why they failed, performed poorly or succeeded, they are uncertain about their ability to avoid failure or repeat success in the future. When students feel uncertain control over their ability to avoid failure or repeat success, the ground is fertile for self-defeating protective behaviour. To build control, students must identify the causes of their failure, poor performance and success. When students know why they failed or performed poorly, they are in a stronger position to avoid it happening again. When students know why they succeeded, they are more likely to repeat that success in the future.

18

EMPOWERING BELIEFS ABOUT CAUSE AND EFFECT

What caused that?

Students' beliefs about cause and effect are referred to as 'causal attributions'. Causal attributions refer to the reasons students have for their success, failure or poor performance. Students' attributions can influence how they behave in the future. There has been much research into attributions that has investigated many of their component dimensions. This chapter focuses on two: locus and controllability.

Locus refers to whether students' success, failure or poor performance is caused by them (internal locus) or by other people and factors (external locus). If they flunked the test because they did not study, then the cause is internal – it was the students themselves who are the cause. If students flunked the test because the teacher is an unfair marker, then the cause is external.

The controllability of success, failure or poor performance refers to students' sense of control over whether they succeed, fail or perform poorly. If they flunked the test because they did not study, then that cause is controllable – it is up to students whether they study or not. If students flunk the test because the teacher is an unfair marker, then that is not within the students' control.

Using locus and controllability as core themes, we can classify all the factors students see as causing their successes, failures or poor performances. The following table shows various possible causes of students' success, failure or poor performance.

Effort and hard work are internal and controllable causes of success, failure or poor performance. Intelligence is an internal cause that is seen by most people to be uncontrollable. Luck, circumstances and performance conditions are examples of causes of outcomes that are external and relatively uncontrollable.

Cause	Outcomes	
	Failure or poor performance	Success
Internal and more controllable	'I failed because of –: – little study – insufficient preparation – not trying – procrastination'	'I succeeded because of –: – hard work – practice – dedication – commitment'
Internal and less controllable	'I failed because I am –: – not competent or clever enough'	'I succeeded because I am –: – clever and competent'
External and less controllable	'I failed because of –: – bad luck – difficult exam – unfair marking'	'I succeeded because of –: – good luck – easy exam – generous marking'

How causal attributions affect students' behaviour

Students' causal attributions for their successes, failures or poor performances determine how they behave next time they are required to perform. Take the case of failure. Students tend to feel powerless when they see the cause of their failure as less controllable and/or external to them (e.g. due to bad luck or an unfair test). On the other hand, students tend to feel more empowered, optimistic and in control when they see the cause of their failure or poor performance as due to factors that are internal and controllable (e.g. hard work, practice, determination, commitment).

Thus, if students attribute the cause of their failure or poor performance to the fact that they are unlucky (i.e. uncontrollable), then they are putting themselves in a difficult position. Essentially, they are saying that the reason they have failed is due to something that is uncontrollable. Students may therefore be pessimistic about how they will perform in the next test. When students are pessimistic about their ability to avoid failure or poor performance, they become tempted to manoeuvre so that failure or poor performance do not look so bad. Unfortunately, this manoeuvring often guarantees failure or poor performance, but students will have made it a more dignified failure.

> Rob, age 16, has not been performing very well at school and he believes the reason for this is because he is not smart enough. Because his competence is something that he sees as fixed and nothing he can improve on, he feels there is little he can do to overcome his poor performance. Rob therefore aims to fail in the most dignified fashion that he can. He starts going out mid-week, getting home late at night, and arriving at school late and clearly fatigued. Sure enough, his performance at school suffers even more, but his poor performance is seen to be because of his late nights and not due to his inability to do the schoolwork. Rob has muddied the waters and in doing so, his poor performance at school is not proof of his incompetence – at least for now.

Students also feel powerless when they see that the causes of their poor performance is due to factors that are external to them. As one student put it, 'I can work my butt off but I still think I'll fail if someone wants me to fail. Just because I work hard won't guarantee that I'll get a good mark'.

> How much control does Miranda, age 15, feel in the next round of tests when the teacher who unfairly failed her last time is the same one marking again? She feels there is little she can do to help her case. This is because the factor she believes is the reason for her last failed attempt (the teacher who was unfair in the last exam) is external to her and something over which she has little or no control. She reacts to this by neglecting her schoolwork and doing little to assist her cause. Why does she engage in such self-defeating behaviour? Because she believes her success, failure and poor performance are externally caused and she has resigned herself to the fact that she may fail again. Essentially, she has become helpless. Helplessness is reflected in low effort, low persistence, poor self-esteem and pessimism. Also, by not trying, her next failed exam can be blamed on the fact that she did not try and not on the fact that she may be incompetent in some way. By preserving her competence image – even though she fails – she has kept her self-esteem intact – at least for a while.

A better way to think about things

If it is external and/or uncontrollable factors that can lay the foundation for further failure or poor performance, then it is internal and controllable factors that empower students. What are the best examples of internal and controllable factors? There are three:

1. effort (how hard students work)
2. strategy (how they do that work)
3. attitude (what they think of themselves, school, schoolwork and teachers)

These factors are internal because they are things students do rather than things that are done to them. These factors are controllable because students decide how much of them they expend. When students attribute the causes of their failure or poor performance to insufficient effort, they greatly enhance their control over improving their performance in the next exam or debate or sporting meet and they are optimistic about future performances.

Take the case of Rob again. He believes the reason for his poor performance at school is because he lacks the competence to do the schoolwork. Because he sees his competence as something he is stuck with and cannot change, he feels powerless and expects to continue to perform poorly. Consequently, he engaged in self-handicapping that enabled him to perform poorly with dignity. Now consider what would happen if he saw that at least part of the reason he performs poorly is because of insufficient effort, poor work practices and inefficient time management. Because these are within his control, he would feel empowered and optimistic, not helpless.

Again, take the case of Miranda. She attributed her failed exam to her teacher's unfair marking. Because she cannot directly control her teacher's marking, she feels powerless to do anything to change the result in the upcoming round of exams and gives up trying. She becomes helpless. How would the outcome change if she attributed the cause of her last failed exam to effort? Let us say that after her last failed exam, she scrutinized her answers and concluded that in addition to tough marking another reason she did not pass was because her answers often had spelling and formatting mistakes in them and were poorly presented. Spelling, formatting and presentation are within her control and something she can change with sufficient effort. Rather than give up trying, she tries harder and makes sure all her exam answers are written and presented to the best of her ability.

Now, this is not to suggest that Miranda's teacher is not an unfair marker. Indeed, there may have been a good degree of unfairness in the grade she received. But by focusing on her teacher as the only reason for failure, she is powerless and may set up another failure. On the other hand, by focusing on what things she can do to change the next outcome, Miranda is empowered and more optimistic. If after Miranda invested enormous effort in her schoolwork and still failed the exam, then she may have to decide whether her efforts would be valued more highly in other subjects or with another teacher. Essentially, then, while it is critical to focus on the factors that are within her control, Miranda must also recognize when her circumstances are so prohibitive that no amount of effort will suffice.

Causal attributions in students' lives

Students would be surprised at the number of factors that they think are beyond their control are actually not beyond their control. There are some students who, if they felt the examiner was unfair (something many of us would see as beyond our control), would seek these examiners out, find out exactly what they expected, and what they could do to do better in the next exam. In the long run, these students often do better than the other students because they refuse to let even apparently external and uncontrollable causes of past failure or poor performance stand between them and success.

In summary, then, the reasons students believe they failed (and succeeded) influence how they behave in the future. What are the reasons your students have for past failures or poor performances? What do they believe was the cause of that failure or poor performance?

- Was it because they were not good enough?
- Was it because the task was too difficult?
- Was it because of some unfairness or injustice?
- Was it because of inadequate assessment?
- Was it because of poor or difficult conditions?

If students believe that they are not good enough, and they see that their competence is pretty much unchangeable, then they will feel there is little they can do in the future to overcome future failure or poor performance. If students tend to see their failures or poor performances as due to external factors such as unfairness, poor conditions or difficult tasks, then there is little these students feel they can do to avoid failure or poor performance in the future.

Attribution retraining

The good news is that students can change the way they see the causes of their successes, failures or poor performances. The trick is to learn to identify the factors underlying academic outcomes that students can control. There have been a number of studies in education that seek to change the way students look at the causes of their success and failure. These studies identify students who attribute their poor performance to factors beyond their control. It is these students who are at most risk of failing again because they see there is nothing they can do to overcome future failure or poor performance.

Researchers have found that they can train these students to learn to see the causes of their poor performance as due to insufficient effort (e.g. not trying hard enough or poor study strategies/techniques). When students see their failure or poor performance as being caused by insufficient effort or poor study strategies, then overcoming failure or poor performance in the future is seen as possible – they must try harder or learn to study more effectively. When students see that overcoming failure or poor performance can be achieved by trying harder or studying more effectively, they are empowered, in control, and optimistic about the future. On the other hand, when students believe that failure and poor performance are due to factors beyond their control or because they are just dumb, then they do not believe failure can be overcome. Students then feel powerless, lacking in control and pessimistic about the future. Research has shown that these students eventually give up trying altogether.

Teacher Tip 20

Encourage students to see the causes of success, failure or poor performance in terms of factors that are within their control (e.g. effort, strategy, attitude) rather than factors over which they have little control

---

Conclusion

When students learn to attribute the causes of outcomes to factors that are within their control (e.g. effort, strategy, attitude), they are in a stronger position to overcome adversity and the challenges before them. As a consequence, students are optimistic and feel empowered in their academic lives. When this is the case, they are not inclined to engage in self-defeating protective behaviours – they are oriented to success seeking.

19
TEACHER TIP
WRAP-UP

This book focuses on success, fear and failure in the classroom, and what teachers can do about them. Part 1 looked at achievement evolution, academic survival in the classroom, how achievement gaps between students occur, and the roles of success, fear and failure in this. Part 2 focused on success seeking, its characteristics, its causes, and its positive consequences. Part 3 examined the many forms of fear and failure in students' academic lives. Part 3 also unpacked the motive for self worth and the lengths students will go to protect their worth in situations of academic threat.

In Part 4, 20 Teacher Tips were developed for building classroom success and reducing fear and failure. Because these are the primary means by which self-defeating behaviour can be addressed in the classroom, they are presented again below. Teachers will need to exercise sound and frank judgement as to which ones are most relevant to their students and classroom. For some, only a few points may be relevant. For other teachers, perhaps all are relevant.

Teacher Tip 1: Show students how failure and poor performance can provide important information about how they can do better next time.

Teacher Tip 2: Help students understand that failure and poor performance say a lot about how hard they try, the way they do things, and their knowledge – and these can be improved.

Teacher Tip 3: Set challenging but realistic 'success zones' (the range of performance that indicates success) for upcoming schoolwork. Then with each success, set students' success zone a little higher.

Teacher Tip 4: Encourage students to expand their view of success to include the process gains (e.g. improvement, personal bests (PBs), skill development, new understanding) they make in their academic lives.

Teacher Tip 5: Encourage students to see that their fundamental worth as a person is not dependent on their ability to perform; rather, their performance reflects more on their effort, strategy and attitude.

Teacher Tip 6: Show students that their effort, strategy and attitude are much sounder bases for their self-esteem than their cleverness – importantly, effort, strategy and attitude can be improved at any time.

Teacher Tip 7: In students' academic lives, there is both a need for mastery and a need for competitiveness. PBs are a great way to coordinate the two. Reducing comparisons with others is also important.

Teacher Tip 8: Show students how their performance very much depends on their prior mastery and not so much on their competitiveness.

Teacher Tip 9: Show students how thinking differently about competition (e.g. as reflecting on mastery and effort rather than competence) can help them deal more effectively with competitive environments and situations.

Teacher Tip 10: Through a focus on mastery, process outcomes, (PBs), and recognizing students' fundamental worth, educators can reshape learning environments to reduce negative effects of competition.

Teacher Tip 11: Teach students how to recognize environments and situations that might trigger a fear of failure and encourage them to focus more on the work to be accomplished and mastery of that work – and less on how their work will be evaluated or compared to someone else.

Teacher Tip 12: Encourage students to understand that focusing on mastery and improvement promotes a success focus and minimizes fear of failure and self-defeating behaviour.

Teacher Tip 13: Show students that for any given competence or skill, they have room to move – upwards and downwards – and they have much control over this.

Teacher Tip 14: Teach students that competence and skills are developed through effort (how hard they work), strategy (how they do that work) and attitude (what they think about themselves, school, schoolwork and teachers).

Teacher Tip 15: Encourage students to minimize the extent to which their feelings about themselves are based on others' responses to them, others' evaluations of them, or their ability to be competent all the time.

Teacher Tip 16: Make it clear to students that while it is nice to have others' approval (or avoid their disapproval), it is not a measure of their worth.

Teacher Tip 17: Encourage students to develop more personal and intrinsic reasons for doing their schoolwork. These reasons can involve satisfaction through mastery, desire for problem solving, development of new skills, striving for personal excellence, or the search for new understanding.

Teacher Tip 18: When students succeed, fail or perform poorly and they do not know why, encourage them to find out why, with particular focus on what is in their control. This enhances their optimism for repeating that success or avoiding that failure or poor performance next time.

Teacher Tip 19: When students receive feedback on their schoolwork, it is essential that they link this feedback to their behaviour (i.e. link their result to how hard they tried, the way they presented their work etc.). This feedback must also be followed up with clear information about what they can do to improve their performance or repeat their success.

Teacher Tip 20: Encourage students to see the causes of success, failure or poor performance in terms of factors that are within their control (e.g. effort, strategy, attitude) rather than factors over which they have little control.

20

GOOD TEACHER-STUDENT RELATIONSHIPS

The success of Teacher Tips 1–20 will very much depend on the quality of teacher–student relationships in the classroom. If the teacher–student relationship is a good one, then the Teacher Tips will hit the mark. If the relationship is not so good, then students are less likely to be receptive to positive strategies implemented by the teacher. The teacher–student relationship, then, forms a very vital backdrop to building classroom success and eliminating fear and failure. In fact, poor teacher–student relationships can directly fuel fear and failure. Hence, not only is a poor relationship a barrier to implementing the Teacher Tips, but they can be the source of the very problems the Tips are designed to combat.

The impact of teacher–student relationships

There is a great deal of research demonstrating the effects of teacher–student relationships on numerous aspects of students' academic outcomes. Here, I briefly discuss some of the research my colleagues and I have conducted in this area. This research has looked at the impact of teacher–student relationships, parent–child relationships and peer relationships on students' academic outcomes. The many factors we assessed included motivation, engagement, behaviour and emotion. The following table summarizes findings for our study on the impact of relationships of more than 3,000 high school students. This table indicates strong (correlations above r=.50), moderate (.30 to .50), slight (.10 to .30) and negligible (around zero) effects.

These results show that the teacher–student relationship has the most substantial impact on students' motivation, engagement, behaviour and emotion in the academic context, followed by parents, and then same-sex peers. As can be seen, a lot of students' motivation, engagement, and other academic orientations are explained by the teacher and the parents.

For example, just taking the strong effects into account, high-quality teacher–student relationships are associated with *greater*:

- self-belief
- valuing of school
- learning focus
- study management
- persistence
- class participation

- enjoyment of school
- positive academic intentions
- personal excellence striving

And, high-quality teacher–student relationships are associated with *lower*:

- disengagement

On the one hand, these are encouraging findings. It shows that teachers have a significant impact on students' motivation and engagement. It shows that investing in the teacher–student relationship will have academic yields for students. It shows that over and above parent and peer effects, teachers have a significant influence. This is important to know in those situations where it seems as though home and peer factors are undermining any good work done by the school and its teachers. These findings show that even if there is a negative effect of home factors, teachers still matter. The findings are also encouraging because they show that peers are not the only influence in a student's academic life. In fact, quite the contrary: at the time of greatest 'stress and storm' in an individual's young life (i.e. adolescence), teachers and parents still have a significant impact on academic outcomes.

On the other hand, these are challenging findings. They are challenging because they indicate the potential price to pay for not getting the relationship right. Not only is a big opportunity to motivate a student lost if the relationship is not going well, but a poor relationship can actually lead to negative academic out-comes. In other words, the positive effects of a good teacher–student relationship are reversed if the teacher–student relationship is of poor-quality. Thus, a poor quality relationship does not lead to a neutral outcome, it actually leads to a negative one.

STUDENTS' RELATIONSHIP WITH ...				
	TEACHER	PARENT	SAME-SEX PEER	OPPOSITE-SEX PEER
Motivation and engagement				
Self-belief	✓✓✓	✓✓	✓✓	✓
Valuing school	✓✓✓	✓✓	✓	0
Learning focus	✓✓✓	✓✓	✓	0
Planning	✓✓	✓✓	✓	0
Study management	✓✓✓	✓✓	✓	0
Persistence	✓✓✓	✓✓	✓	0
Anxiety	0	0	–	–
Fear of failure	–	–	–	–
Uncertain control	– –	–	–	–
Self-handicapping	– –	–	–	0
Disengagement	– – –	– –	– –	0
Behaviour and affect				
Homework completion	✓✓	✓	✓	0
Weeks absent from school	–	–	0	0
Class participation	✓✓✓	✓	✓✓	✓
Enjoy school	✓✓✓	✓✓	✓✓	✓
Positive intentions	✓✓✓	✓✓	✓	0
Personal excellence	✓✓✓	✓✓	✓	✓
Academic buoyancy	✓✓	✓	✓✓	✓

Notes
✓✓✓ for strong positive effect or – – – for strong negative effect
✓✓ for moderate positive effect or – – for moderate negative effect
✓ for slight positive effect or – for slight negative effect
0 for negligible effect

Characteristics of good teacher–student relationships

If a high-quality teacher–student relationship is so pivotal to students' academic outcomes, what are the characteristics of such relationships? Here I draw on a government report I compiled summarizing the findings of a review conducted into boys' education. In this review I led focus groups and interviews with boys and girls looking at many aspects of school life. One key consideration related to the qualities and characteristics of teachers who most effectively engaged students academically. Importantly, the questions posed to students revolved around their academic engagement and development. Hence, I was not so interested in teachers who were fun to be around but who did not progress their students academically. Nor was I interested in discussing teachers who knew a lot about their subject but were not able to connect with the students. Instead, I was very interested in teachers that seemed to get all these dimensions right.

In total, I identified 12 characteristics or practices that were consistently noted as reasons why some teachers were able to engage students in their schoolwork while other teachers were not so effective at doing so. They are as follows:

1. Good interpersonal connectedness
2. The teacher's enjoyment of teaching and working with young people
3. Striking a balance between authority and a relaxed classroom atmosphere
4. Striking a balance between serious schoolwork and fun
5. A sense of humour
6. Making schoolwork interesting and fun where possible and appropriate
7. Providing students with choices
8. A youthful teaching style (irrespective of age)
9. Being something of an 'all-round' teacher
10. Explaining work clearly and effectively and aiming for mastery by all students
11. Broad assessment practices
12. Variety in teaching material and teaching methods.

I briefly address each in turn.

Particularly critical to students' engagement and motivation in a school subject was the *interpersonal connectedness* between teacher and student. These were characterized by the teacher taking time to get to know students, listening to students, respecting their views, and not demeaning them:

- 'They know how you're feeling'.
- 'He knows you a bit better, knows the way you work and that sort of stuff, so he can help you a bit more'.
- 'She knows what your motivations are, she gets you to do stuff. Like in science I was talking at the beginning of the year and she moved my friend and I up the front of the class away

from our other friends so our work improved. There were no distractions and we listened to everything the teacher said'.

Teachers who related well to students and who also engaged them seemed to *enjoy teaching and working with young people*:

- 'They just like working with children and they like what they're doing'.
- 'You can tell if they are really interested in it. Some teachers just talk about the facts and they don't have any enthusiasm'.
- 'I like a teacher that enjoys helping kids'.

Good teacher–student relationships were characterized by a *good balance* between maintaining authority and creating a relaxed and well-behaved classroom atmosphere:

- 'Keeps the class under control but not too strict'.
- 'Has a joke with you, but knows when it's time to get down to work and chat a bit more then do some more work'.
- 'She can be a fun-going teacher but she can be strict with the work as well'.

High-quality teacher–student relationships were also reflected in a *sense of humour* and an ability to share this with students by laughing at students' jokes or sharing jokes of their own. These teachers could also tolerate a bit of fun poked at them and could poke a bit of fun back:

- 'Some teachers will laugh at a joke that others would get angry at'.
- 'Tells jokes and laughs at jokes and fits in with the class'.
- 'They joke around with you . . . and pay out on you. If you pay them out, they'll pay out back. That's good'.

These teachers were also seen to take the time to try to *make schoolwork interesting and fun where possible*. This was recognized and appreciated by the students:

- 'They're animated, walk around the class and give demonstrations and help students. They make it interesting'.
- 'They will try to motivate us and get us interested. Like in Shakespeare we were bored, but they got us into it by getting us to act out a full scene and that was pretty fun'.
- 'The teacher we have in English tells us why different ways of saying things in the old days makes more understanding of

how to talk and write essays today – it wouldn't be interesting otherwise'.

Teachers who *provided students with choices* were particularly valued. Choices gave students some ownership of what they were studying and also provided them with a sense that the teacher respected them:

– 'Last year I was in an English class where our teacher let us choose what books we did and how we did them. It was really good'.

A *youthful and dynamic teaching style* was also consistently cited by students as being an important factor that contributed to a good teacher–student relationship and academic engagement. Importantly, students recognized that it was a youthful teaching style rather than the age of a teacher that was the key factor. According to one student:

– 'We had a couple of great 'fossil' teachers and they were really great to be around'.

One of the keys to a youthful teaching style was that these teachers could remember their own youth and time at high school:

– 'Personally I found a few teachers who seem to relate and seem to be able to remember back when they were in high school'.

Interpersonally connected teachers were also seen to be *'all-rounders'*, addressing students' varying needs, keeping control of the class yet injecting humour and fun appropriately, and making material clearly relevant:

– 'Creative or fun-going, extremely creative, extremely helpful and helps us do things that are going to be beneficial to our future. On the other hand, he is strict with the due dates'.
– 'To be an all-round teacher, not be one person who like goes in one area or full-on makes all hard work for the kids. Manages to plot everything around and helps all areas of students. Like if they're not so good at subjects she makes it fun for them to learn'.

Connected and engaging teachers also *explained work carefully* to students and *aimed for mastery by all students*. In many cases this required individualized attention and students found this helpful:

189

- 'They get you into the work. They help you out. They explain it to you before you do it. They give you a bit more attention'.

Students seemed to benefit from *broad assessment practices* that assessed them in a number of different areas and gave them a chance to be assessed in areas of strength:

- 'Our English teacher marked everyone differently. Like, he'd mark one person on a PowerPoint presentation and another person on essays'.

Providing *variety in teaching material and method* was also considered important by some students:

- 'Varying some of the work would be good. Instead of just writing a huge block about a subject, kind of mixing it around'.

To sum up, students were readily able to identify the key characteristics and practices of teachers that underpinned a quality teacher–student relationship, engaged them most, and enhanced their learning. Among the most consistently cited factors were: good interpersonal connectedness between teacher and student, the teacher's enjoyment of teaching and working with young people, the teacher striking a good balance between asserting authority and being relaxed and tolerant, injecting and permitting humour in the classroom, providing students with choices, making schoolwork interesting and/or relevant, a youthful and dynamic teaching style (irrespective of the teacher's age), providing variety in content and methods, and respecting students' opinions and perspectives.

Connective instruction

Having identified these elements of quality teacher–student relationships, the vital question is this: how can teachers *immediately* build these relatedness factors into their teaching practice? Particularly in high school, teachers do not have a few spare weeks to solely dedicate to building interpersonal connections with students. The curriculum is simply too crowded and the realities of accountability in schools means that there is not a lot of time to play with. It is therefore important to hook interpersonal connectedness into pedagogy as it occurs on a day-to-day basis. 'Connective instruction' is a framework I have developed to help do this.

I define connective instruction as pedagogy that connects to the student on three levels:

1. the level of substance and subject matter
2. the interpersonal level
3. the pedagogical level

Essentially, then, connective instruction comprises three key relationships:

1. the substantive relationship (the connection between the student and the subject matter and substance of what is taught)
2. the interpersonal relationship (the connection between the student and the teacher)
3. the pedagogical relationship (the connection between the student and the pedagogy/teaching)

It is therefore evident that a great lesson can be likened to a great musical composition, comprising the song (the substantive), the singer (the interpersonal) and the singing (the pedagogy). When the student connects in all three ways, there is a solid foundation for high-quality engagement in the teaching and learning context. Essentially, then, it is proposed that pedagogy has the greatest capacity to enhance motivation, engagement and achievement when the individual student personally connects to the substance and subject matter, the teacher and the teaching. This proposed connective instruction framework is presented in the following figure.

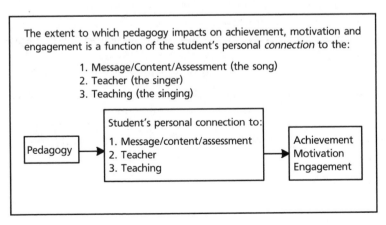

The extent to which pedagogy impacts on achievement, motivation and engagement is a function of the student's personal *connection* to the:

1. Message/Content/Assessment (the song)
2. Teacher (the singer)
3. Teaching (the singing)

Pedagogy →

Student's personal connection to:
1. Message/content/assessment
2. Teacher
3. Teaching

→ Achievement Motivation Engagement

The interpersonal relationship (the singer)

The first key connection is that between the student and the teacher. In previous research I have identified key characteristics of good interpersonal relationships in the teaching and learning context. These include:

- actively listening to students' views
- allowing student input into decisions that affect them
- getting to know the students
- affirming all students and showing no favouritism
- accepting students' individuality
- having positive but attainable expectations for students

It is suggested that these elements characterize high-quality interpersonal relationships. These are an important means by which the student engages with the 'who' of the teaching and learning context.

The substantive relationship (the song)

The second key connection is that between the student and the actual subject matter, the substance, and the nature of tasks conducted in the teaching and learning context. My research has identified core elements of substance and subject matter that facilitate students' connection to the teaching and learning context. These include:

- setting work that is challenging but not too difficult
- assigning work that is important and significant
- building variety into content and assessment tasks
- assigning interesting work
- drawing on material that is fun to learn, where possible and appropriate
- utilizing material and assigning tasks that arouse curiosity

It is suggested that these elements reflect content, subject matter and learning tasks to which an individual student can meaningfully connect. These are an important means by which the student engages with the 'what' of the teaching and learning context.

The pedagogical relationship (the singing)

The third key connection is that between the student and the teaching or pedagogy itself. I have articulated some key elements of effective pedagogy including:

- maximizing opportunities for students to succeed and develop competence
- providing clear feedback to students focusing on how they can improve
- explaining things clearly and carefully
- injecting variety into teaching methods
- encouraging students to learn from their mistakes
- clearly demonstrating to students how schoolwork is relevant and/or meaningful
- ensuring all students keep up with the work and allowing for opportunities to catch up

It is suggested that these elements characterize high-quality pedagogy. These are an important means by which the student engages with the 'how' of the teaching and learning context.

Self-audit of connective instruction

It is possible for teachers to conduct a self-audit of the status of connective instruction in their own teaching practice. The following three tables show checklists of the key elements of each of the three parts of connective instruction. In each table, the teacher assesses whether a given element is a strength or a weakness. A tally of responses provides a quick indication of the nature of the connective instruction conducted by that teacher. It also provides a quick indication as to which of the three cornerstones of connective instruction reflects the teacher's strength and which of the three cornerstones are suggestive of the need for further development.

The first table shows the students' relationship with the teacher ('the singer'), the second table shows the students' relationship with the message/content/assessment ('the song'), and the third table shows the students' relationship with the teaching/pedagogy ('the singing').

Interpersonal Relationship	STRENGTH 'I do this well and it is a part of my regular practice'	NOT APPLICABLE/ RELEVANT/ IMPORTANT	WEAKNESS I don't do this very much or very well'
	TICK ONE (✓)		
I make an effort to listen to my students' views			
A good teacher–student relationship is one of my priorities			
I give my students input into things and decisions that affect them			
I enjoy working with young people			
Where appropriate I try to have a sense of humour with my students			
I get to know my students			
I explain the reasons for rules that are made and applied			
I show no favouritism			
I accept my students' individuality			
I have positive but attainable expectations for students			
TALLY			

Substantive Relationship	STRENGTH 'I do this well and it is a part of my regular practice'	NOT APPLICABLE/ RELEVANT/ IMPORTANT	WEAKNESS I don't do this very much or very well'
		TICK ONE (✓)	
I set work that is challenging but not too difficult			
Where possible, I set work that is important and significant			
I inject variety into my teaching content			
I inject variety into my assessment tasks			
I provide students with interesting work			
I use broad and authentic (relevant and meaningful) assessment			
I try to ensure that my teaching content is not boring to young people			
In class and assigned work, I reduce monotony as much as possible			
Where possible I draw on material that is fun to learn			
Where possible I use material that arouses my students' curiosity			
TALLY			

Pedagogical Relationship	STRENGTH 'I do this well and it is a part of my regular practice'	NOT APPLICABLE/ RELEVANT/ IMPORTANT	WEAKNESS I don't do this very much or very well'
	TICK ONE (✓)		
I get students to do something well as much as possible and provide support needed to do this			
I have multiple indicators of success in schoolwork (marks, effort, reaching goals, improvement)			
I provide clear feedback to students focusing on how they can improve			
I make an effort to explain things clearly and carefully			
I inject variety into my teaching methods and reduce repetition or monotony			
I encourage my students to learn from their mistakes			
I aim for mastery by all students			
I show students how schoolwork is relevant and/or meaningful			
I make sure all students keep up with work and give opportunities to catch up or go over difficult work			
I don't rush my lessons or my explanations			
TALLY			

Conclusion

The teacher–student relationship makes a real difference to students' motivation, engagement and achievement. Indeed, this chapter has also shown that teachers have an impact on students' academic motivation and engagement as much as or greater than parents and peers. Moreover, the many comments provided in this chapter by students themselves show that students have a very good idea of the attributes and characteristics that reflect high-quality teacher–student relationships and teachers' ability to engage them.

The extent to which students are receptive to Teacher Tips 1–20 will very much depend on teachers' capacity to deliver pedagogy in a way that enables the individual student to connect in personally meaningful ways to three key elements of that pedagogy: the substance of what is taught (the song), how it is taught (the singing), and who is doing the teaching (the singer). These, it is proposed, are the three cornerstones of connective instruction – instruction that maximizes students' personal connections in the teaching and learning context. When students are more personally connected with the teaching and learning context, they are more engaged and motivated to work and achieve to their potential.

This chapter, then, is the capstone to the 20 Teacher Tips detailed in this book. Teacher–student relationships are the foreground and background to building success in the classroom. In the absence of good relationships, classroom success is limited. Where negative relationships prevail, so do fear and failure. Where teacher–student relationships flourish, so do student and classroom success.

21
CONCLUSION

This book has emphasized that the classroom is one of the most important places where students have the opportunity to learn the skills, attributes and characteristics to achieve in a changing world. Classrooms that are geared to success and assist students to achieve are the classrooms that will best prepare students for achievement in a changing world. Classrooms characterized by fear and failure risk limiting students' potential and capacity to thrive in the world.

Teachers can do an excellent job of helping students work to their personal potential, preparing them for success in a changing and variable world. Teachers can nurture individuality and help students succeed in many and varied ways. Teachers can cultivate a group climate where failure and poor performance do not destabilize students' progress. Teachers can help students take the lessons to be learnt from poor performance and assist them to then move onwards and upwards. Teachers can nurture an atmosphere where fear is not the dominant dynamic in the classroom. Through these practices, teachers can place students in their classroom on positive achievement trajectories.

This book has presented detailed advice and information on how to build classroom success and eliminate fear and failure. It is appropriate to also endorse some big picture principles that are valuable backdrops for any specific teaching and instruction.

- *Expect more of students*: The expectations teachers hold for students are powerful. Positive expectations tell students that teachers believe in them and what students can aim for. Positive expectations therefore also underpin academic progress.
- *Different students respond in different ways*: For some students, the impact of the strategies in this book will be dramatic. For other students, the effect may be more subtle and it may appear as though they have not changed much. Do not underestimate subtle changes. Students can tuck an idea away and draw on it at the most unexpected times. Moreover, a small shift now can lay the groundwork for significant changes later.
- *If students do not 'succeed', this does not mean they are bad people*: Try not to fall into the trap of connecting students' achievement to their worth as a person. It is important to send positive messages to students about their worth as a person

even though they may not be making you very happy from a motivation or achievement perspective.

- *Do not expect yourself to be perfect* (but look for opportunities to do better): Teachers will get things wrong sometimes and react or behave in ways that do not reflect a positive approach. When this happens teachers need to own it and then look to deal with things better next time.
- *Every student has strengths*: I have yet to find a student who is a 'failure' on every conceivable academic measure. Each student has some glimmers of strength and these are the windows through which to enhance other parts of that student's academic life. Try not to lose sight of students' strengths – they are the launch pad for success.
- *Good students need to be sustained*: When we focus on struggling students (as we should), it is easy to forget that good students also need to be sustained. This means identifying strong students' strengths, the reasons why they are strengths, and the ways to maintain these strengths – and then look to build them further.
- *Different advice and strategy will suit different students*: Different students are suited to different messages and strategies. Teachers (not me) will know their students best and what is realistic and achievable when aiming to boost their academic fortunes. This also means that teachers can adapt or change strategies to better suit their own teaching style and their students' learning style.
- *Do fewer things well rather than too many things not so well*: It is not realistic to expect teachers to do all that has been presented in this book. Instead of spreading too thin across many strategies, aim to focus and do a good job on a smaller and more manageable number of strategies.
- *There is usually no magic answer*: Students (as with all human beings) are complex creatures and expecting quick and simple answers is not realistic. Fundamental and substantial change takes time and is not necessarily easy. More often than not, improving educational outcomes takes time, energy, flexibility, and a commitment over the medium to longer term.
- *You can lead a horse to water, and although you cannot make it drink, you can salt the oats to make it thirsty:* Teachers cannot study for their students and cannot force students to do something if students really do not want to do it. However,

teachers can certainly create the conditions for students to be more interested in learning and more willing to put in some hard work. Thus, even though teachers cannot make the horse drink, they can salt the oats to make it thirsty. This book is focused on creating conditions in the classroom and shaping situations to make students thirsty to achieve to their personal potential.

- *Ongoing professional development*: To keep up with students and the world in which they live, it is important to upgrade skills and knowledge on an ongoing basis. Not only do students develop over the course of a year and the course of school life, but curriculum undergoes constant change, assessment demands change, school organization and structures change, old staff leave and new staff arrive, and government or departmental policy is constantly on the move. To survive and thrive through this flux, teachers need to regularly assess, reassess, and adjust their teaching practices and teaching philosophies.

Promoting success and eliminating fear and failure are pivotal to students' achievement in the classroom and their capacity to achieve well beyond their school years. Teachers substantially contribute to students' achievement evolution through school, students' academic fitness, and students' capacity to recognize and seize the opportunities of the twenty-first century. In short, teachers make a significant difference in students' academic and non-academic lives.

I wish you well as you positively shape your students' life course.

Bibliography

Abramson, L.Y., Seligman, M.E.P., & Teasdale, J. (1978). Learned helplessness in humans: Critique and reformulation. *Journal of Abnormal Psychology, 87,* 49–74.

Ames, C., & Archer, J. (1988). Achievement goals in the classroom: Students' learning strategies and motivation processes. *Journal of Educational Psychology, 80,* 260–267.

Arkin, R.M., & Oleson, K.C. (1998). Self-handicapping. In J.M. Darley & J. Cooper (Eds). *Attribution and social interaction: The legacy of Edward E. Jones.* Washington, DC: American Psychological Association.

Atkinson, J.W. (1957). Motivational determinants of risk-taking. *Psychological Review, 64,* 359–372.

Bandura, A. (1997). *Self-efficacy: The Exercise of Control.* New York: Freeman & Co.

Bandura, A. (2006). Adolescent development from an agentic perspective. In F. Pajares & T. Urdan (Eds). *Self-efficacy Beliefs.* CO: Information Age Press.

Baumeister, R.F., & Scher, S.J. (1988). Self-defeating behaviour patterns among normal individuals: Review and analysis of common self-destructive tendencies. *Psychological Bulletin, 104,* 3–22.

Bempechat, J., London, P., & Dweck, C.S. (1991). Children's conceptions of ability in major domains: An interview and experimental study. *Child Study Journal, 21,* 11–36.

Berglas, S. (1990). Self-handicapping: Etiological and diagnostic considerations. In R.L. Higgins, C.R. Snyder., & S. Berglas (Eds). *Self-handicapping: The Paradox that Isn't.* New York: Plenum Press.

Bobis, J., Anderson, J., Way, J., & Martin, A.J. (in press). A model for mathematics instruction to enhance student motivation and engagement. In D.J. Brahier (Ed.). *Motivation and Disposition: Pathways to Learning Mathematics.* Reston, VI: National Council of Teachers of Mathematics (NCTM).

Borba, M. (1989). *Esteem Builders*. New York: Jalmar.

Borba, M. (1996). *Self-esteem: A Classroom Affair*. San Francisco: Harper.

Brophy, J (1997). *Motivating Students to Learn*. Boston, MA: McGraw-Hill.

Brophy, J.E. (1996). *Teaching Problem Students*. New York: Guilford.

Burgess, R. (2000). *Laughing Lessons: 149 Ways to Make Teaching and Learning Fun*. Minneapolis: Free Spirit Publications.

Canfield, J., & Wells, C. (1993). *100 Ways to Enhance Self-Concept in the Classroom*. Upper Saddle River, NJ: Prentice Hall.

Canfield, J., & Wells, C. (1994). *100 Ways to Enhance Self-Concept in the Classroom: A Handbook for Teachers, Counsellors, and Group Leaders*. Boston, MA: Allyn & Bacon.

Cantor, N., & Norem, J.K. (1989). Defensive pessimism and stress and coping. *Social Cognition, 7*, 92–112.

Carr-Gregg, M. (2004) *Surviving Year 12*. Sydney: Finch Publishing.

Ceil, C. (1994). *Motivating Underachievers: 172 Strategies for Success*. Australia: Hawker Brownlow Education.

Coleman, J., & Hagell, A. (2007) (Eds). *Adolescence, Risk, and Resilience: Against the Odds*. London: John Wiley & Sons.

Connell, J.P. (1985). A new multidimensional measure of children's perceptions of control. *Child Development, 56*, 1018–1041.

Covington, M.V. (1992). *Making the Grade: A Self-Worth Perspective on Motivation and School Reform*. Cambridge: Cambridge University Press.

Covington, M.V. (1998). *The Will to Learn: A Guide for Motivating Young People*. New York: Cambridge University Press.

Covington, M.V., & Beery, R.G. (1976). *Self-worth and School Learning*. New York: Holt, Rinehart & Winston.

Dalgleish, T. (1999). *Self-esteem: Lower Primary*. Glebe: Blake Education.

Dalgleish, T. (1999). *Self-esteem: Upper Primary*. Glebe: Blake Education.

Deci, E.L., & Ryan, R.M. (2000). The darker and brighter sides of human existence: Basic psychological needs as a unifying concept. *Psychological Inquiry, 11*, 319–338.

Dewey, J. (1916). *Democracy and Education*. New York: Macmillan.

Diener, C.I., & Dweck, C.S. (1980). An analysis of learned helplessness II. The processing of success. *Journal of Personality and Social Psychology, 39,* 940–952.

Dixon, R.M., Craven, R.G., & Martin, A.J. (2006). Underachievement in a whole city cohort of academically gifted children: What does it look like? *Australasian Journal of Gifted Education, 15,* 9–15.

Duda, J.L. (1993). Goals: A social-cognitive approach to the study of achievement motivation in sport. In R.N. Singer., M. Murchey., & L.K. Tennant (Eds). *Handbook of Research on Sport Psychology.* New York: Macmillan.

Dweck, C.S. (1986). Motivational processes affecting learning. *American Psychologist, 41,* 1040–1048.

Dweck, C.S., & Leggett, E.L. (1988). A social-cognitive approach in motivation and personality. *Psychological Review, 95,* 256–273.

Elliot, A.J., & Church, M.A. (1997). A hierarchical model of approach and avoidance achievement motivation. *Journal of Personality and Social Psychology, 72,* 218–232.

Feather, N.T. (1967). Level of aspiration and performance variability. *Journal of Personality and Social Psychology, 6,* 37–46.

Finn, J.D., & Rock, D.A. (1997). Academic success among students at risk for school failure. *Journal of Applied Psychology, 82,* 221–234.

Fredrickson, B.L. (2001). The role of positive emotions in positive psychology. *American Psychologist, 56,* 218–226.

Fried-Buchalter, S. (1992). Fear of success, fear of failure, and the impostor phenomenon: A factor analytic approach to convergent and discriminant validity. *Journal of Personality Assessment, 58,* 368–379.

Fry, G., & Martin, A.J. (1994). Factors contributing to identification and incidence of stress during the school practicum as reported by supervising teachers. In T.A. Simpson (Ed.). *Teacher Educators' Annual Handbook.* Queensland: QUT Press.

Fuller, A. (1998). *From Surviving to Thriving: Promoting Mental Health in Young People.* Melbourne: ACER Press.

Furrer, C., & Skinner, E. (2003). Sense of relatedness as a factor in children's academic engagement and performance. *Journal of Educational Psychology, 95,* 148–162.

Garvin, M., & Martin, A.J. (1999). High school students' part-time employment and its relationship to academic engagement and psychological well-being. *Australian Journal of Guidance and Counselling, 9,* 1–14.

Geary, D.C. (2008). An evolutionarily informed education science. *Educational Psychologist, 43,* 179–195.

Ginsberg, M.B., & Wlodkowski, R.J., (2000). *Creating Highly Motivated Classrooms for all Students: A School-Wide Approach to Powerful Teaching with Diverse Learners.* San Francisco: Jossey-Bass.

Glasser, W. (1998). *The Quality School: Managing Students Without Coercion.* New York: Harper Perennial.

Green, J., Martin, A.J., & Marsh, H.W. (2007). Motivation and engagement in English, mathematics and science high school subjects: Towards an understanding of multidimensional domain specificity. *Learning and Individual Differences, 17,* 269–279.

Green, J., Nelson, G., Martin, A.J., & Marsh, H.W. (2006). The causal ordering of self-concept and academic motivation and their effects on academic achievement. *International Education Journal, 7,* 534–546.

Harackiewicz, J.M., Barron, K.E., & Elliot, A.J. (1998). Rethinking achievement goals: When are they adaptive for college students and why? *Educational Psychologist, 33,* 1–21.

Harris, R.N., & Snyder, C.R. (1986). The role of uncertain self-esteem in self-handicapping. *Journal of Personality and Social Psychology, 51,* 451–458.

Harter, S., & Connell, J.P. (1984). A model of children's achievement and related self-perceptions of competence, control, and motivation orientation. In J. Nicholls (Ed.). *The Development of Achievement Motivation.* London: JAI Press.

Hattie, J. (2009). *Visible Learning: A Synthesis of Over 800 Meta-analyses Relating to Achievement.* Oxford: Routledge.

Hawkes, T. (2001). *Boy oh Boy.* Frenchs Forest: Pearson Education Australia.

Heacox, D. (1991). *Up from Underachievement: How Teachers, Students, and Parents Can Work Together to Promote Student Success.* Minneapolis: Free Spirit Publications.

Higgins, R.L. (1990). Self-handicapping: Historical roots and contemporary branches. In R.L. Higgins, C.R. Snyder., & S. Berglas (Eds). *Self-handicapping: The Paradox that Isn't.* New York: Plenum Press.

Holt, J. (1982). *How Children Fail.* New York: Penguin.

Jackson, S.A., Martin, A.J., & Eklund, R.C. (2008). Long and short measures of flow: Examining construct validity of the FSS-2, DFS-2, and new brief counterparts. *Journal of Sport and Exercise Psychology, 30,* 561–587.

Jagacinski, C.M., & Nicholls, J.G. (1987). Competence and affect in task-involvement and ego-involvement: The impact of social comparison information. *Journal of Educational Psychology, 79,* 107–114.

Jensen, W.R., Rhode, G., & Reavis, H.K. (1994). *The Tough Kid Tool Box.* Frederick, CO: Sopris West.

Johnson, D.W., & Johnson, R.T. (1989). *Cooperation and Competition: Theory and Research.* Minnesota: Interaction.

Johnson, D.W., & Johnson, R.T. (2008). Social interdependence theory and cooperative learning: The teacher's role. In R.M. Gillies, A. Ashman, & J. Terwel (Eds), *The Teacher's Role in Implementing Cooperative Learning in the Classroom* (pp. 9–36). New York, NY: Springer.

Jones, E.E., & Berglas, S. (1978). Control of attributions about the self through self-handicapping strategies: The appeal of alcohol and the role of underachievement. *Personality and Social Psychology Bulletin, 4,* 200–206.

Kernis, M.H., Grannemann, B.D., & Barclay, L.C. (1992). Stability of self-esteem: Assessment, correlates, and excuse making. *Journal of Personality, 60,* 621–644.

Keyes, C.L.M. (2007). Promoting and protecting mental health as flourishing. *American Psychologist, 62,* 95–108.

Killen, R. (1998). *Effective Teaching Strategies.* Katoomba: Social Science Press.

Leary, M.R., & Shepperd, J.A. (1986). Behavioural self-handicaps versus self-reported handicaps: A conceptual note. *Journal of Personality and Social Psychology, 51,* 1265–1268.

Linfoot, K., Martin, A.J., & Stephenson, J. (1999). Preventing conduct disorder: A study of parental behaviour management and support needs with children aged 3–5 years. *International Journal of Disability, Development, and Education, 46,* 223–246.

Lovitt, T.C. (2000). *Preventing School Failure: Tactics for Teenage Adolescents.* Texas: pro-ed.

Maehr, M.L. (1984). Meaning and motivation. In R. Ames & C. Ames (Eds), *Research in Motivation: Vol. 1. Student Motivation* (pp. 115–144). Lexington, MA: D.C. Heath.

Mansour, M., & Martin, A.J. (in press). Home, parents, and achievement motivation: A study of key home and parental factors that predict student motivation and engagement. *Australian Educational and Developmental Psychologist.*

Manzino, R.J. (2003). *What Works in Schools.* Alexandria, VA: ASCD.

Marsh, H.W. (2007). *Self-concept Theory, Measurement and Research into Practice: The Role of Self-Concept in Educational Psychology.* Leicester, UK: British Psychological Society.

Marsh, H.W., Cheng, J., & Martin, A.J. (2008). How we judge ourselves from different perspectives: Contextual influences on self-concept formation. In M. Maehr., T. Urdan., & S. Karabenick (Eds). *Advances in Motivation and Achievement.* Vol. 15. New York: Elsevier.

Marsh, H.W., Craven, R. G., & Martin, A.J. (2006). What is the nature of self-esteem? Unidimensional and multidimensional perspectives. In M. Kernis (Ed.). *Self-esteem: Issues and Answers.* New York: Psychology Press.

Marsh, H.W., Martin, A.J., & Cheng, J. (2008). A multilevel perspective on gender in classroom motivation and climate: Potential benefits of male teachers for boys? *Journal of Educational Psychology, 100,* 78–95.

Marsh, H.W., Martin, A.J., & Debus, R. (2001). Individual differences in verbal and math self-perceptions: One factor, two factors, or does it depend on the construct? In R. Riding & S. Rayner (Eds). *International Perspectives on Individual Differences.* London: Greenwood Publishing.

Marsh, H.W., Martin, A.J., & Hau, K.T. (2006). A multiple method perspective on self-concept research in educational psychology: A construct validity approach. In M. Eid & E. Diener (Eds). *Handbook of Multimethod Measurement in Psychology.* Washington, DC: American Psychological Association Press.

Marsh, H.W., Papaioannou, A., Martin, A.J., & Theodorakis, Y. (2006). Motivational constructs in Greek physical education classes: Factor structure, gender and age effects in a nationally representative longitudinal sample. *International Journal of Sport and Exercise Psychology, 4,* 121–148.

Marsh, H.W., Rowe, K., & Martin, A.J. (2002). PhD students' evaluations of research supervision: Issues, complexities and challenges in a nationwide Australian experiment in benchmarking universities. *Journal of Higher Education, 73,* 313–348.

Martin, A.J. (1999). Assessing the multidimensionality of the 12-item General Health Questionnaire. *Psychological Reports, 84,* 927–935.

Martin, A.J. (2001). The Student Motivation Scale: A tool for measuring and enhancing motivation. *Australian Journal of Guidance and Counselling, 11,* 1–20.

Martin, A.J. (2002). Motivating the gifted and talented: Lessons from research and practice. *Australasian Journal of Gifted Education, 11,* 26–34.

Martin, A.J. (2002). Motivation and academic resilience: Developing a model of student enhancement. *Australian Journal of Education, 46,* 34–49.

Martin, A.J. (2002). The lethal cocktail: Low self-belief, low control, and high fear of failure. *Australian Journal of Guidance and Counselling, 12,* 74–85.

Martin, A.J. (2003). Boys and motivation: Contrasts and comparisons with girls' approaches to schoolwork. *Australian Educational Researcher, 30,* 43–65.

Martin, A.J. (2003). Burning to learn. *Principal Matters, 56,* 14–16.

Martin, A.J. (2003). Enhancing the educational outcomes of boys: Findings from the A.C.T. investigation into boys' education. *Youth Studies Australia, 22,* 27–36.

Martin, A.J. (2003). *How to Motivate your Child for School and Beyond.* Sydney: Bantam.

Martin, A.J. (2003). The relationship between parents' enjoyment of parenting and children's school motivation. *Australian Journal of Guidance and Counselling, 13,* 115–132.

Martin, A.J. (2003). The role of significant others in enhancing the educational outcomes and aspirations of Indigenous/Aboriginal students. *Aboriginal Studies Association Journal, 12,* 23–26.

Martin, A.J. (2003). The Student Motivation Scale: Further testing of an instrument that measures school students' motivation. *Australian Journal of Education, 47,* 88–106.

Martin, A.J. (2004). Perplexity and passion: Further consideration of the role of positive psychology in the workplace. *Journal of Organizational Behaviour Management, 24,* 203–205.

Martin, A.J. (2004). School motivation of boys and girls: Differences of degree, differences of kind, or both? *Australian Journal of Psychology, 56,* 133–146.

Martin, A.J. (2004). The role of positive psychology in enhancing satisfaction, motivation, and productivity in the workplace. *Journal of Organizational Behaviour Management, 24,* 113–133.

Martin, A.J. (2005). Exploring the effects of a youth enrichment program on academic motivation and engagement. *Social Psychology of Education, 8,* 179–206.

Martin, A.J. (2005). *How to Help your Child Fly Through Life: The 20 Big Issues.* Sydney: Bantam.

Martin, A.J. (2005). The Student Motivation and Engagement Wheel – 'Researcher in Profile' section. In D. McInerney & V. McInerney (Eds). *Educational Psychology: Constructing Learning* (4th Edition). Sydney: Prentice Hall.

Martin, A.J. (2006). A motivational psychology for the education of Indigenous students. *Australian Journal of Indigenous Education, 35,* 30–43.

Martin, A.J. (2006). Pastoral pedagogy: When learning makes beautiful music. *Leadership in Focus, 4,* 7–9.

Martin, A.J. (2006). Personal bests (PBs): A proposed multi-dimensional model and empirical analysis. *British Journal of Educational Psychology, 76,* 803–825.

Martin, A.J. (2006). The relationship between teachers' perceptions of student motivation and engagement and teachers' enjoyment of and confidence in teaching. *Asia-Pacific Journal of Teacher Education, 34,* 73–93.

Martin, A.J. (2007). Examining a multidimensional model of student motivation and engagement using a construct validation approach. *British Journal of Educational Psychology, 77,* 413–440.

Martin, A.J. (2008). Enhancing student motivation and engagement: The effects of a multidimensional intervention. *Contemporary Educational Psychology, 33,* 239–269.

Martin, A.J. (2008). How domain specific are motivation and engagement across school, sport, and music? A substantive-methodological synergy assessing young sportspeople and musicians. *Contemporary Educational Psychology, 33,* 785–813.

Martin, A.J. (2008). Motivation and engagement in diverse performance domains: Testing their generality across school, university/college, work, sport, music, and daily life. *Journal of Research in Personality, 42,* 1607–1612.

Martin, A.J. (2008). Motivation and engagement in music and sport: Testing a multidimensional framework in diverse performance settings. *Journal of Personality, 76,* 135–170.

Martin, A.J. (2009). Age appropriateness and motivation, engagement, and performance in high school: Effects of age-within-cohort, grade retention, and delayed school entry. *Journal of Educational Psychology, 101,* 101–114.

Martin, A.J. (2009). Motivation and engagement in the workplace: Examining a multidimensional framework from a measurement and evaluation perspective. *Measurement and Evaluation in Counseling and Development, 41,* 223–243.

Martin, A.J. (2009). Motivation and engagement across the academic lifespan: A developmental construct validity study of elementary school, high school, and university/college students. *Educational and Psychological Measurement 69,* 794–824.

Martin, A.J. (in press). Multidimensional motivation and engagement: The Motivation and Engagement Wheel – 'Researcher in Profile' section. In D. McInerney (Ed.). *Educational Psychology: Constructing Learning* (5th Edition). Sydney: Pearson.

Martin, A.J. (in press). Physical activity motivation in late adolescence: Refinement of a recent multidimensional model. *Research Quarterly for Exercise and Sport.*

Martin, A.J. (in press). Should students have a gap year? Motivation and performance factors relevant to time out after completing school. *Journal of Educational Psychology.*

Martin, A.J., Colmar, Davey, L., & Marsh, H.W. (in press). Longitudinal modeling of academic buoyancy and motivation: Do the '5Cs' hold up over time? *British Journal of Educational Psychology.*

Martin, A.J., & Debus, R.L. (1998). Self-reports of mathematics self-concept and educational outcomes: The roles of ego-dimensions and self-consciousness. *British Journal of Educational Psychology, 68,* 517–535.

Martin, A.J., & Debus, R.L. (1999). An alternative factor structure for the Revised Self-Consciousness Scale. *Journal of Personality Assessment, 72,* 266–281.

Martin, A.J., & Dowson, M. (2009). Interpersonal relationships, motivation, engagement, and achievement: Yields for theory, current issues, and practice. *Review of Educational Research, 79,* 327–365.

Martin, A.J. & Liem, G.A. (in press), Academic Personal Bests (PBs), engagement, and achievement: A cross-lagged panel analysis. *Learning and Individual Differences.*

Martin, A.J., Linfoot, K., & Stephenson, J. (1999). How teachers respond to concerns about misbehaviour in their classroom. *Psychology in the Schools, 36,* 347–358.

Martin, A.J., Linfoot, K., & Stephenson, J. (2000). Exploring the cycle of mother-child relations, maternal confidence, and children's aggression. *Australian Journal of Psychology, 52,* 34–40.

Martin, A.J., Linfoot, K., & Stephenson, J. (2005). Problem behaviour and associated risk factors in young children. *Australian Journal of Guidance and Counselling, 15,* 1–16.

Martin, A.J. & Jackson, S.A. (2008). Brief approaches to assessing task absorption and enhanced subjective experience: Examining 'Short' and 'Core' flow in diverse performance domains. *Motivation and Emotion, 32,* 141–157.

Martin, A.J., & Marsh, H.W. (2003). Fear of failure: Friend or foe? *Australian Psychologist, 38,* 31–38.

Martin, A.J., & Marsh, H.W. (2005). Motivating boys and motivating girls: Does teacher gender really make a difference? *Australian Journal of Education, 49,* 320–334.

Martin, A.J., & Marsh, H.W. (2006). Academic resilience and its psychological and educational correlates: A construct validity approach. *Psychology in the Schools, 43,* 267–282.

Martin, A.J., & Marsh, H.W. (2008). Academic buoyancy: Towards an understanding of students' everyday academic resilience. *Journal of School Psychology, 46,* 53–83.

Martin, A.J., & Marsh, H.W. (2008). Workplace and academic buoyancy: Psychometric assessment and construct validity amongst school personnel and students. *Journal of Psychoeducational Assessment, 26,* 168–184.

Martin, A.J., & Marsh, H.W. (2009). Academic resilience and academic buoyancy: Multidimensional and hierarchical conceptual framing of causes, correlates, and cognate constructs. *Oxford Review of Education, 35,* 353–370.

Martin, A.J., Marsh, H.W., & Debus, R.L. (2001). A quadripolar need achievement representation of self-handicapping and defensive pessimism. *American Educational Research Journal, 38,* 583–610.

Martin, A.J., Marsh, H.W., & Debus, R.L. (2001). Self-handicapping and defensive pessimism: Exploring a model of predictors and outcomes from a self-protection perspective. *Journal of Educational Psychology, 93,* 87–102.

Martin, A.J., Marsh, H.W., & Debus, R.L. (2003). Self-handicapping and defensive pessimism: A model of self-protection from a longitudinal perspective. *Contemporary Educational Psychology, 28,* 1–36.

Martin, A.J., Marsh, H.W., Debus, R.L. & Malmberg, L-E. (2008). Performance and mastery orientation of high school and university/college students: A Rasch perspective. *Educational and Psychological Measurement, 68,* 464–487.

Martin, A.J., Marsh, H.W., McInerney, D.M., & Green, J. (2009). Young people's interpersonal relationships and academic and non-academic outcomes: The relative salience of teachers, parents, same-sex peers, and opposite-sex peers. *Teachers College Record,* March, http://www.tcrecord.org.

Martin, A.J., Marsh, H.W., McInerney, D.M., Green, J., & Dowson, M. (2007). Getting along with teachers and parents: The yields of good relationships for students' achievement motivation and self-esteem. *Australian Journal of Guidance and Counselling, 17,* 109–125.

Martin, A.J., Marsh, H.W., Williamson, A., & Debus, R.L. (2003). Self-handicapping, defensive pessimism, and goal orientation: A qualitative study of university students. *Journal of Educational Psychology, 95,* 617–628.

Martin, A.J., Marsh, H.W., Williamson, A., & Debus, R.L. (2005). Fear of failure in students' academic lives: Exploring the roles of self-handicapping and defensive pessimism from longitudinal, multidimensional, and qualitative perspectives. In H.W Marsh., R.G. Craven., & D.M. McInerney (Eds). *International Advances in Self Research.* Vol 2. Greenwich, CT: Information Age Publishing.

Martin, A.J., Milne-Home, J., Barrett, J., & Spalding, E. (1997). Stakeholder perceptions of the institution: To agree or not to agree. *Journal of Institutional Research in Australasia, 6,* 53–67.

Martin, A.J., Milne-Home, J., Barrett, J., Spalding, E., & Jones, G. (2000). Graduate satisfaction with university and perceived employment preparation. *Journal of Education and Work, 13,* 199–214.

Martin, A.J., & Smith, I. (1997). Television violence: A review and suggested longitudinal model. *Australian Journal of Social Issues, 32,* 407–430.

Martin, A.J., Tipler, D.V., Marsh, H.W., Richards, G.E., &

Williams. M.R. (2006). Assessing multidimensional physical activity motivation: A construct validity study of high-school students. *Journal of Sport and Exercise Psychology, 28,* 171–192.

Martz, L. (1992). *Making School Better.* Times Books.

McClelland, D.C. (1965). Toward a theory of motive acquisition. *American Psychologist, 20,* 321–333.

McCombs, B.L. (1997). *The Learner-centered Classroom and School: Strategies for Increasing Student Motivation and Achievement.* San Francisco, CA: Jossey-Bass.

McElherne, L.N. (1999). *Jump Starters: Quick Classroom Activities that Develop Self-esteem, Creativity and Cooperation.* Minneapolis, MI: Free Spirit Publications.

McGuire, J.V., & Heuss, B. (1995). *Bridges: A self-esteem Activity Book for Students in Grades 4–6.* Boston, MA: Allyn & Bacon.

McInerney, D. (2000). *Helping Kids Achieve their Best.* Sydney: Allen & UnwIn

Meece, J.L., Blumenfeld, P.C., & Hoyle, R.H. (1988). Students' goal orientation and cognitive engagement in classroom activities. *Journal of Educational Psychology, 80,* 514–523.

Middleton, C., Marsh, H.W., Martin, A.J., Richards, G., Savis, J., Perry, C., & Brown, R. (2004). The Psychological Performance Inventory: Is the mental toughness test tough enough? *International Journal of Sport Psychology, 35,* 91–108.

Midgley, C., Arunkumar, R., & Urdan, T.C. (1996). 'If I don't do well tomorrow, there's a reason': Predictors of adolescent's use of academic self-handicapping strategies. *Journal of Educational Psychology, 88,* 423–434.

Mitchell, C., & Espeland. (1996). *Teach to Reach: Over 300 Strategies, Tips, and Helpful Hints for Teachers of All Grades.* Minneapolis, MI: Free Spirit Publishing.

Munns, G., Martin, A.J., & Craven, R. (2008). To free the spirit? Motivation and engagement of Indigenous students. *Australian Journal of Indigenous Education, 37,* 98–107.

Murphy, P.K., & Alexander, P.A. (2000). A motivated exploration of motivation terminology. *Contemporary Educational Psychology, 25,* 3–53.

Nicholls, J.G. (1989). *The Competitive Ethos and Democratic Education.* Cambridge: Harvard University Press.

Noble, C., & Bradford, W. (2000). *Getting it Right for Boys ... and Girls.* London: Routledge.

Norem, J.K., & Cantor, N. (1986). Defensive pessimism: Harnessing anxiety as motivation. *Journal of Personality and Social Psychology, 51*, 1208–1217.

Norem, J.K., & Illingworth, K.S.S. (1993). Strategy-dependent effects of reflecting on self and tasks: Some implications of optimism and defensive pessimism. *Journal of Personality and Social Psychology, 65*, 822–835.

Orlick, T. (1982). *The Second Cooperative Sports and Games Book.* NY: Pantheon Books.

Parker, P.D., & Martin, A.J. (2008). Personal capacity building for the human services: What is the relative salience of curriculum and individual differences in predicting self-concept amongst college/university students? *Learning and Individual Differences, 18*, 486–491.

Parker, P.D., & Martin, A.J. (2009). Coping and buoyancy in the workplace: Understanding their effects on teachers' work-related well-being and engagement. *Teaching and Teacher Education, 25*, 68–75.

Parker, P.D., Martin, A.J., & Marsh, H.W. (2008). Factors predicting life satisfaction: A process model of personality, multidimensional self-concept, and life satisfaction. *Australian Journal of Guidance and Counselling, 18*, 15–29.

Parker, P.D., Martin, A.J., Martinez, C., Marsh, H.W., & Jackson, S.A. (in press). Stages of change in physical activity: A validation study of late adolescents. *Health Education and Behaviour.*

Patrick, B.C., Skinner, E.A., & Connell, J.P. (1993). What motivates children's behaviour and emotion? Joint effects of perceived control and autonomy in the academic domaIn *Journal of Personality and Social Psychology, 65*, 781–791.

Patrick, H., Ryan, A.M., & Kaplan, A. (2007). Early adolescents' perceptions of the classroom social environment, motivational beliefs, and engagement. *Journal of Educational Psychology, 99*, 83–98.

Perry, R.P., Magnusson, J.L., Parsonson, K.L., & Dickens, W.J. (1986). Perceived control in the college classroom: Limitations in instructor expressiveness due to noncontingent feedback. *Journal of Educational Psychology, 78*, 96–107.

Peterson, C., Maier, S.F., & Seligman, M.E.P. (1993). *Learned Helplessness: A Theory for the Age of Personal Control.* New York: Oxford University Press.

Piaget, J. (1970). *The Science of Education and the Psychology of the Child.* New York: Orion Press.

Pintrich, P.R. (2003). A motivational science perspective on the role of student motivation in learning and teaching contexts. *Journal of Educational Psychology, 95,* 667–686.

Pyszczynski, T., & Greenberg, J. (1983). Determinants of reduction in intended effort as a strategy for coping with anticipated failure. *Journal of Research in Personality, 17,* 412–422.

Relich, J., Way, J., & Martin, A.J. (1994). Attitudes to teaching mathematics: Further development of a measurement instrument. *Mathematics Education Research Journal, 6,* 56–69.

Rhodewalt, F. (1990). Self-handicappers: Individual differences in the preference for anticipatory, self-protective acts. In R.L. Higgins, C.R. Snyder., & S. Berglas (Eds). *Self-handicapping: The Paradox that Isn't.* New York: Plenum Press.

Riggs, J.M. (1992). Self-handicapping and achievement. In A.K. Boggiano & T.S. Pittman (Eds). *Achievement and Motivation: A Social-developmental Perspective.* Cambridge University Press.

Rizzo Toner, P. (1993). *Stress Management and Self-esteem Activities.* NY: Center for Applied Research in Education.

Robb, J., & Letts, H. (2000) *Succeed in Exams. Triumph in Tests.* Sydney: Hodder.

Roeser, R.W., Midgley, C., & Urdan, T.C. (1996). Perceptions of the school psychological environment and early adolescents' psychological and behavioural functioning in school: The mediating role of goals and belonging. *Journal of Educational Psychology, 88,* 408–422.

Rosenberg, M. (1986). Self-concept from middle childhood through adolescence. In J. Suls & A.G. Greenwald (Eds). *Psychological Perspectives on the Self.* Hillsdale, NJ: Erlbaum.

Roseth, C.J., Johnson, D.W., & Johnson, R.T. (2008). Promoting early adolescents' achievement and peer relationships: The effects of cooperative, competitive, and individualistic goal structures. *Psychological Bulletin, 134,* 223–246.

Rutter, M. (2006). *Genes and behaviour: Nature-nurture interplay explained.* London: Blackwell Publishing.

Ryan, R.M., & Deci, E.L. (2000). Self-determination theory and the facilitation of intrinsic motivation, social development, and well-being. *American Psychologist, 55,* 68–78.

Scheier, M.F., & Carver, C.S. (1985). The Self-consciousness Scale: A revision for use with general populations. *Journal of Applied Social Psychology, 15,* 687–699.

Schunk, D.H. (1983). Ability versus effort attributional feedback:

Differential effects on self-efficacy and achievement. *Journal of Educational Psychology, 75,* 848–856.

Seligman, M.E.P. (1995). *The Optimistic Child: A Revolutionary Approach for Raising Resilient Children.* Sydney: Random House.

Shepperd, J.A., & Arkin, R.M. (1989). Self-handicapping: The moderating roles of public self-consciousness and task importance. *Personality and Social Psychology Bulletin, 15,* 252–265.

Sher, B. (1998). *Self-esteem Games: 300 Fun Activities that Make Children Feel Good About Themselves.* NY: John Wiley.

Showers, C. (1988). The effects of how and why thinking on perceptions of future negative events. *Cognitive Therapy and Research, 12,* 225–240.

Skaalvik, E.M. (1990). Attribution of perceived academic results and relations with self-esteem in senior high school students. *Scandinavian Journal of Educational Research, 34,* 259–269.

Skinner, E.A. (1996). A guide to constructs of control. *Journal of Personality and Social Psychology, 71,* 549–570.

Slavin, R.E. (1996). Research on cooperative learning and achievement: What we know, what we need to know. *Contemporary Educational Psychology, 21,* 43–69.

Snyder, C.R. (1990). Self-handicapping: Processes and sequelae – on the taking of a psychological dive. In R.L. Higgins, C.R. Snyder., & S. Berglas (Eds). *Self-handicapping: The Paradox that Isn't.* New York: Plenum Press.

Speirs, T., & Martin, A.J. (1999). Depressed mood amongst adolescents: The roles of perceived control and coping style. *Australian Journal of Guidance and Counselling, 9,* 55–76.

Stanovich, K.E. (1986). Matthew effects in reading: Some consequences of individual differences in the acquisition of literacy. *Reading Research Quarterly, 21,* 360–406.

Stephenson, J., Linfoot, K., & Martin, A.J. (1999). Dealing with problem behaviour in young children: Teacher use and preferences for resources and support. *Special Education Perspectives, 8,* 3–15.

Stephenson, J., Linfoot, K.W., & Martin, A.J. (2000). How teachers of young children respond to problem behaviour in the classroom. *Australasian Journal of Special Education, 24,* 21–31.

Stephenson, J., Martin, A.J., & Linfoot, K. (2005). Promoting positive interactions between mothers and their at-risk young children. *Australian Journal of Educational and Developmental Psychology, 5,* 128–137.

Stipek, D.J. (1997). *Motivation to Learn: From Theory to Practice.* Boston: Allyn & Bacon.

Stipek, D.J., & Gralinski, J.H. (1996). Children's beliefs about intelligence and school performance. *Journal of Educational Psychology, 88,* 397–407.

Sweller, J. (2004). Instructional design consequences of an analogy between evolution by natural selection and human cognitive architecture. *Instructional Science, 32,* 9–31.

Thompson, T. (1994). Self-worth protection: Review and implications for the classroom. *Educational Review, 46,* 259–274.

Tice, D.M. (1991). Esteem protection or enhancement? Self-handicapping motives and attribution differ by self-esteem. *Journal of Personality and Social Psychology, 60,* 711–725.

Urdan, T.C., Midgley, C., & Anderman, E.M. (1998). The role of classroom goal structure in students' use of self-handicapping strategies. *American Educational Research Journal, 35,* 101–122.

Van der Kley, M. (1991). *Cooperative Learning – and How to Make it Happen in Your Classroom.* NZ: Purse Willis & Aiken.

Walker, D., & Brown, P. (1994). *Pathways to Co-operation: Starting Points for Co-operative Learning.* Sydney: Eleanor Curtain

Watson, K., & Martin, A.J. (1996). The role of attitude in intercultural understanding: An assessment of secondary students' freehand maps. In N.L. Baumgart (Ed.). *Changing the Landscape: Cultures and Environments in Curriculum.* Sydney: Pacific Circle Consortium for Education.

Weiner, B. (1994). Integrating social and personal theories of achievement striving. *Review of Educational Research, 64,* 557–573.

Winebrenner, S. (2001). *Teaching Gifted Kids in the Regular Classroom.* Minneapolis, MI: Free Spirit Publishing.

Withers, G., & Russell, J. (2001). *Educating for Resilience: Prevention and Intervention Strategies for Young People at Risk.* Melbourne: ACER Press.

Index